Congratulations
on a wonderful life
together and a new
beginning.
love,
Chris & Katie Curtis

Marriage &
Family: Gospel
Insights

Marriage & Family: Gospel Insights

Stephen R. Covey
and
Truman G. Madsen

Bookcraft

Salt Lake City, Utah

Library of Congress Catalog Card Number: 83-62419
ISBN O-88494-503-0

6th Printing, 1994

Lithographed in the United States of America
PUBLISHERS PRESS
Salt Lake City, Utah

To our grandchildren

Contents

Preface   ix

Truman G. Madsen

1   Looking Forward and Backward   3

2   The Roots of Family in Judaism   10

3   Jesus and the Family   15

4   Love   20

5   Love at Home   27

6   Tests of Circumstances   33

7   Temple and Home   41

8   Church and Family Callings   51

9   The Self   57

10   The Real Family   63

11   The Little Things   70

12   Solving, Resolving, and Dissolving   75

13   What It Means to Be Sealed   87

14   Peace   90

Stephen R. Covey

15   The Supreme Importance of an Eternal Perspective   95

16   Our Scripts Come from People, Not from Principles   99

17   Four Divine Scripting Models   108

18   Two Goals: P and PC   112

19   Three Roles: Producer, Manager, and Leader   121

20   Brain Dominance Theory and the Three Roles   130

21   Three Bermuda Triangles   140

22   Four Family Systems: Goal Selection and Planning   145

23   Four Family Systems: Teaching and Training   153

24   Four Family Systems: Communication and Problem-Solving Systems   167

25   Four Family Systems: The Stewardship/Discipline System   173

26   Three Critical Skills in Producing, Managing, and Leading   191

27   The Communication Skill   198

28   The Problem-Solving Skill   209

29   Seven Sources of Internal Security   224

Index   235

Preface

We did not write this book. We were, instead, encouraged to "workshop" it. In a series of marathon seminars, each four hours in length, we have, as laymen, gathered and presented material revolving around family life and the gospel. The communication process has been, as we kept pleading, "two way." Hundreds of responses have come to us, many of them in writing. Our notes and transcripts have been honed, restructured, and in some parts dropped. What is presented here is the heart of the melon.

These sources and resources are designed both for maintenance and for overhaul. Where there has been shipwreck, they are for "rebuilding the ship at sea." They presuppose readers who share our ultimate and intimate commitment. They will make little sense otherwise.

In the workshops, as in our writing, we divided the material into two main categories: (1) "Why" questions—questions on the meaning of marriage and family life in an eternal perspective; (2) "How" questions—the nitty-gritty of ways and means. But we have learned anew that the division is artificial. Our exposure to real people in the heavy seas of matrimony reconfirms it: Nothing is more practical, nothing more down to earth, than the gospel. "Tinkering with the machinery" when that perspective is lacking is, sooner or later, futile. On the other hand, to be blessed with the vision of possibilities without workable modes of procedure can itself be defeating.

As will appear, we have great respect for trained practitioners of the family sciences, particularly for the many well-trained and dedicated family counselors within the Mormon community. (For example, see Victor L. Brown, Jr., *Human Intimacy: Illusion and Reality*, Parliament Publishers, 1981.) We have equal regard for firsthand experience, the experience of an increasing number of couples and children whose souls are on fire with the "divine center."

We have learned by experience that there is constant need for recurrence to basics. Over and over we find people drained and haunted and pulled in many directions who ask in anguish and sometimes in bitterness, "What's it all about?" Getting back toward the trunk of the tree revitalizes as well as renews. Both of us witness, with so many others, that such renewal is most rich, most powerful, and most effective in the environs of the temple, which we here call a "model home."

Much of what we say here has to do with the relation of man and wife and less of parents to children. There are two reasons for this: If there can be a solid relationship between parents and the Lord, most of the problems with the children will be resolvable. Second, the fundamental principles of the gospel apply to all human relationships.

Because of the phrase "Physician, heal thyself," at times we have felt to withdraw from a realm overloaded with advice. Yet we ourselves have cried "help" and been helped. And the concern has been so continuing, the discoveries so moving, and the benefits so meaningful in our own families, that we have kept at it.

We realize that marriage and family questions are highly personal, and that each person is at a different stage of development. Does the gospel have a pat answer to each of our dilemmas? We are saying rather that the gospel is terribly relevant and that, properly understood and applied, it solves our problems; but exactly how it applies in each individual life and each individual case frequently is for the person or couple to work out, seeking inspiration from the Lord. The gospel provides the plan whereby such imperatives may be found.

The approaches we make here have been helpful to us. They are neither absolute nor final. Both of us want to avoid helps that are hindrances. And both of us are committed to another principle of the gospel that is often overlooked in an advice-oriented age: The beginning of help is self-help. No one should be overdependent on anyone or anything. Each person needs to recognize that if he has problems they are *his* problems. The application of the gospel to individual cases, we repeat, requires both wisdom and inspiration.

The workshops were designed for couples. But singles came all alone and shared their perceptions. Singles are many. They are everywhere. And none of us, whether now married or not, will likely escape joining them at some time or another. That is reality. Then is not such a discussion as this pouring salt and vinegar into their wounds? Our conviction is to the contrary. The gospel teaches that there are no orphans or singles. Regardless of what happens to us, mighty, eternal relationship-strings remain. And, visible or invisible, they are stronger than the cords of death. Like the boy holding the kite string who is asked how he knows it is "up there" when fog and cloud obscure it, we may answer, "I can tell by the pull of it." The assurance is there, even for those of us who doubt it the most.

The discovery, and for Latter-day Saints the rediscovery, that man really belongs to the same family as God, that we share in his same kind of existence, that we are his and he is ours in a bond that only we can break, is "like learning that one has won the sweepstakes." (See Hugh Nibley, "Treasures in the Heavens," *Dialogue*, vol. 8, no. 374, 1973, p. 84.) Regardless of our present status, our Father still lives. We belong. Our belonging can be enhanced in the midst of forced isolation. And our becoming is interrelated to our belonging.

It follows that the keeping of the vision of marriage and family life is crucial for all of us. The solution to a rocky marriage and a disrupted family is not the cynical disparagement of both. It is planting our roots deeper as branches of the tree of life. This is the way around—and even through—the alternative death-styles that surround us.

STEPHEN R. COVEY
TRUMAN G. MADSEN

Truman G. Madsen

for philosophical

Looking Forward
and Backward

T he children of Zion love in proportion to the heavenly knowledge which they have received; for love keeps pace with knowledge, and as the one increases so does the other, and when knowledge is perfected, love will be perfected also." (*The Seer*, p. 156.)

So wrote Orson Pratt a century ago. As if to verify this connection of knowledge and love, his brother, Parley P. Pratt, after receiving "a single glance of eternity" during a revelatory afternoon with the Prophet Joseph Smith, wrote:

> I had loved before, but I knew not why. But now I loved with a pureness, an intensity of elevated, exalted feeling, which would lift my soul from the transitory things of this grovelling sphere and expand it as the ocean. . . . In short, I could now love with the spirit and with the understanding also."

What heavenly knowledge came to him that afternoon? It was the whence and the whither of family life.

We have an outline in Parley's account:

> It was at this time that I received from him [Joseph Smith] the first idea of eternal family organization, and the eternal union of the sexes in those inexpressibly endearing relationships which none but the highly intellectual, the refined and pure in heart, know how to prize, and which are at the very foundation of everything worthy to be called happiness. . . .
>
> It was from him that I learned that the wife of my bosom might be secured to me for time and all eternity; and that the refined sympathies and affections which endeared us to each other emanated from the fountain of divine eternal love. It was from him that I learned that we might cultivate these affections, and grow and increase in the same to all eternity." (*Autobiography of Parley P. Pratt*, 3rd ed., Deseret Book, 1938, pp. 297-98.)

Keep the Vision

The beginning and end of this section of our approach to the family is: "Keep the Vision." Without the vision, marriage perishes.

But at seminars we have been asked, "Why torment us with the celebration of the ideal? In moments of bleak discouragement all we really want is a little hope that we can get through today until sundown. Why dangle before us possibilities which, however beautiful, are disabling in their contrast to where we really are, where we really live, what we really feel?"

Our answer is that the truth about our pasts and futures, when brought into the present, are so brilliant, so emancipating, so motivating, that no other attempt at meeting our needs can compare. This is the unfailing resource. Without some stirring of memory and aspiration toward it, we are of all men most vulnerable. In contrast, an abiding sense of eventual outcome—even without a guarantee as to how soon—"nerves us up," as the Prophet Joseph put it; we can endure and overcome. And we can experience measurable joy along the way.

Others may be more heroic, and even in a strange way more admirable, if they go on living without such perspective, without such divine sanction. But this is hardly a good reason to reject the shining truth. "Whatsoever is truth is light, and whatsoever is light is Spirit, even the Spirit of Jesus Christ" (D&C 84:45). "And if it be in you it shall abound" (D&C 88:66).

The Gospel Framework

Normally we would begin at the beginning, but in this case there wasn't one. Gospel understanding, the logic that springs from it, and the spiritual echoes from the past convince us that family, like love, is not only endless but beginningless.

We all know that somehow marriage is of God. The primal commandment to our first parents was to multiply and replenish the earth. The highest ordinance in the kingdom of God is the sealing of husband and wife. We know too that the ultimate outcome, indeed the only ultimate meaning of the creation of the earth, is the forging of a lasting connection, a living, loving family chain from Adam to the last mortal birth.

But there is a preface to all this. And we can only comprehend the vision of family in this life if we sense something of its origins in a prior life. Origins shed light on destinies.

Elder James E. Talmage wrote:

> The Church of Jesus Christ of Latter-day Saints affirms as reasonable, scriptural, and true, the doctrine of the eternity of sex among the children of God. The distinction between male and female is no condition peculiar to the relatively brief period of mortal life; *it was an essential characteristic of our pre-existent state,* even as it shall continue after death, in both the disembodied and resurrected states. (*Young Woman's Journal,* vol. 25, 1914, pp. 602-3.)

Looking Backward

"The doctrine of pre-existence," the First Presidency wrote, "throws a wonderful light upon the otherwise mysterious problem of man's origin."

Their statement continued:

> It shows that man, as spirit, was begotten and born of heavenly parents, and reared to maturity in the eternal mansions of the Father

prior to coming upon the earth in a temporal body to undergo an experience in mortality.

The Church proclaims man to be the direct and lineal offspring of deity. . . .

All men and women are in the similitude of the universal Father and Mother and are literally sons and daughters of deity. ("Statement of the First Presidency," *Improvement Era*, vol. 28, p. 1090.)

We add to those powerful glimpses four core-certainties provided by Joseph Smith as to the realms of pre-mortality:

1. At the great organization in heaven we were all present and "saw the Savior chosen and appointed and the plan of salvation made and we sanctioned it." (*Teachings of the Prophet Joseph Smith*, p. 181. Hereafter referred to as *Teachings*.)

2. "Every man who has a calling to minister to the inhabitants of the world [does that not include our families?] was ordained to that very purpose in the Grand Council of heaven before this world was" (*Teachings*, p. 365).

3. "The Father called all spirits before Him at the creation of man, and organized them" (*Teachings*, p. 158).

The organization of the spiritual and heavenly worlds, and of spiritual and heavenly beings, was agreeable to the most perfect order and harmony: their limits and bounds were fixed irrevocably, and voluntarily subscribed to in their heavenly estate by themselves, and were by our first parents subscribed to upon the earth. Hence the importance of embracing and subscribing to principles of eternal truth by all men upon the earth that expect eternal life. (*Teachings*, p. 325.)

4. We are "lawful heirs, according to the flesh, and have been hid from the world with Christ in God. . . . Therefore blessed are ye if ye continue [not begin] in my goodness, a light unto the Gentiles, and through this priesthood, a savior unto my people [family] Israel." (D&C 86:9, 11.)

When Brigham Young was concerned with principles of family

relations and when and where adoption should be encouraged, he had a revelatory dream in which he conversed with Joseph Smith. He was told over and over to teach one answer: "Follow the Spirit. Keep the Spirit of the Lord"; to keep their hearts open to that Spirit that whispers peace and joy.

> Joseph then showed me the pattern, how they were in the beginning. This I cannot describe, but I saw it, and saw where the Priesthood had been taken from the earth (and then restored) and how it must be joined together, so that there would be a perfect chain from Father Adam to his latest posterity. Joseph again said, "Tell the people to be sure and keep the Spirit of the Lord and follow it, and it will lead them just right." (Journal History, February 23, 1847.)

And then this promise:

> "If they will, they will find themselves just as they were organized by our Father in Heaven, before they came into the world. Our Father in Heaven organized the human family, but they are all disorganized and in great confusion." (Journal History, February 23, 1847. Published in Preston Nibley's *Exodus to Greatness*, Salt Lake City, Utah, Deseret News Press, 1947.)

The veil has been drawn and we have all become little children. "But," as President Joseph F. Smith wrote, "by the power of the Spirit, in the redemption of Christ, through obedience, we often catch a spark from the awakened memories of the immortal soul, which lights up our whole being as with the glory of our former home." (*Gospel Doctrine*, Deseret Book Co., 1949, p. 14.) There are tuggings and flashes of recognition (re-cognition). And Elder George Q. Cannon said of family kinships:

> There are instances which all of us doubtless have known which have proved to us that there has been a *spiritual acquaintance* existing between us. . . . *We are drawn together* by this knowledge and this acquaintanceship which, I have no doubt, was formed anterior to our birth in this state of existence. (*Gospel Truth*, vol. 1, Deseret Book Co., 1974, p. 4. Italics added.)

Said Elder Orson F. Whitney: "We believe that ties of this world will extend to the next. Why not believe that we had similar ties before we came into this world . . . some of them, at least?" (*Improvement Era* 23:100.)

A diary entry records an expression of the Prophet:

> Wilford Woodruff referred to a saying of Joseph Smith, which he heard him utter [like this] That if the people knew *what was behind the veil* they would try by every means to commit suicide that they might get there, but the Lord in his wisdom had implanted the *fear of death* in every person that they might cling to life and thus accomplish the designs of their creator. (Diary of Charles L. Walker, August, 1877, St. George, p. 596, BYU Special Collections.)

This entry may be the origin of the folklore version that Joseph Smith taught that the glory of the telestial kingdom is such that if we could see it we would take our own lives. It is the glory of the *celestial* kingdom, and perhaps "the glory we had with the Father before the foundation of the world," that it is presently better for us not to remember. Hence "the veil has been drawn."

The Church *does* teach that we are all siblings in the eternal family of God. The Church does *not* teach that the quest for family life is somehow locked into heavy-handed fate or predestination, that we should seek a "soul mate," a "one and only." Free agency is inviolate. And by righteousness we are to help our chosen mate *become.* This is our privilege and our covenant responsibility. We understand, too, that by our "sanction," our valiance, and our responses to Christ in that prior realm we may even have had something to do with the time and circumstances of our mortal probation, our entry into this obstacle course with its abundance of opportunity and risk. All this is clearly taught by the prophets.

Unwanted children as well as unwanted mates can be evaded from what seem the best of motives. In the early days of the Church as today there were some deeply troubled by the incorrigible enmity of their parents for the gospel or for them, or for both. One way out of their frustration was to ask to be "adopted" to someone else.

Each of the presidents of the Church in turn felt that there must be clarification concerning sealing and the laws of adoption. It came to President Wilford Woodruff. He established and announced the principle: "Have children sealed to their parents, and run this chain through as far as you can get it . . . this is the will of the Lord to his people." He added, "It is my duty, to honor my father [who had not joined the Church] who begot me in the flesh. It is your duty to do the same. When you do this, the Spirit of God will be with you." He testified, "There will be very few, if any, who will not accept the gospel. . . . the fathers of this people will embrace the gospel." He added, "They know more in that world than we do here." (See "The Law of Adoption," Discourse of Wilford Woodruff, April 18, 1894, *Utah Genealogical and Historical Magazine,* October 1922, pp. 149-50.) Clearly we are not to trifle with our inheritance.

2

The Roots of
Family in Judaism

Now let us trace one fountainhead of family life—in that surviving religious tradition on which in part we as a people are built. They are more than our cousins—they are us. They have carried the family legacy through millennia, enduring the worst shocks human flesh can endure. I speak of the children of Judah.

The rabbis differ on what it means to say man is "the image and likeness of God." Is it "the moral image" or "the rational image"? or something else? But in Judaism so indelible is that image, and so tied to fatherliness and motherliness, that the failure to perpetuate it "diminishes the image."

In the Hebrew language there is no neuter case, no "it." Grammatically, everything in the cosmos is either masculine or feminine. Jewish lore teaches that man is (of this there are many interpretations) of "one stock" with the Divine. In all of us are "the divine sparks." In one strand of Jewish tradition the glory of the Divine is personified as Schechinah, a female, maternal, queenly, counterpart of God. Symbolically she is separated—or in exile awaiting reunion with the Divine. That reunion is interrelated with the redemption and reunion of all the children of men.

The Midrash teaches that Adam was created with two bodies, one of which was pulled away to create Eve. The reunion with each other—not their final separation from each other—is to bring redemption.

So with all mankind. "What has God been doing since creation?" the Talmud asks. Playfully but also joyfully it answers, "Making marriages." A realistic, perhaps cynical tradition opines that a good marriage is as rare as the parting of the Red Sea. But the faith of Judaism is that there are few misalliances. The glorification of procreation is written into the whole Torah, the manifestation of God in law, as it is in the incredibly rich collection of stories, allegories, and homilies of Judaism.

"Every soul is holy ground," and each man and woman is seen as an infinity. From this derives the implicit horror of murder. If you save a life, you save a race; if you take a life (even by abortion) you destroy a race. Abraham and Sarah are viewed as the mighty prototypes of patriarchal promise. (The promise to Sarah that she would bear a son and the miraculous delivery of Isaac removed every wrinkle and line from her face. She dated her own age from the day of his birth.) Hence the majesty of their willingness to sacrifice before God their only hope of the glory of God—posterity. They say the *akedah* or binding of Isaac was so sublime an act of faith that God turned into a high and sacred mount the flat ground on which Abraham had built the altar.

The promise of posterity given to Abraham was not only numerical but assured the replication of his spiritual qualities. "I can only bless thee with this, that all the trees planted from thy seed may be as noble in every respect as thou art." (Genesis Rabbah 17, *A Treasury of the Midrash*, Samuel Rappaport, New York, KTAV Publishing, 1968, p. 133.)

For Jewish orthodoxy: "Man in celibacy is in sublime ignorance of what is meant by the words good, help, joy, blessing, peace, and expiation of sin. He is in fact, not entitled to the dignified name of man.'' The high priest who was to represent all Israel at the Holy of Holies on the Day of Atonement must have a wife. Only if his heart was permeated by the love of wife and children in the home could he, according to Talmudic law, offer up family prayer to the Universal Father in full expectation that he would be heard.

Woman

Joseph Smith says that in Hebrew the word *ruach* should be translated *spirit* or *breath* when it is applied to Adam, but when it applies to Eve it should be translated *lives. (Teachings,* p. 301.) In Hebrew, *Haveh* (Eve) means life or lives.

In Hebrew sources also Eve and woman are glorified in ways which neither modern secular idealizings nor Christian traditions can match. It was woman's persuasive power, the Midrash says, that led man out of paradise, and it is woman's light that will bring him back. Father is incomprehensible without mother, king without queen. The metaphor of the Sabbath is a "queen," is the culmination and joy-filled outcome of the other six days. The queen of the Sabbath is the mother, the bride, the culmination of man's labors, hopes, and aspirations. For the divine realm as for the human, wedding symbolism abounds. Pagan religious thought, which lapsed into fertility cults, is viewed as a distortion of this sacred truth.

Note these concepts from Midrash literature:

At Sinai, women received and accepted the Decalogue before the men.

"There shall be no man without a woman and no woman without a man, and no man and woman together without God." (Compare Paul in 1 Corinthians 11:11.) (The very Hebrew words for man and woman have implicit within them the word *Yah,* which is a divine name.

If a husband marries a bad woman, he becomes bad. If a woman marries a bad man, he becomes good. Conclusion: Everything depends on woman.

Woman attains discretion at an earlier age than man.

Woman comes from Adam's rib, a modest part, and is not fond of show but of the maternal virtues.

A man should look on the birth of a daughter as a blessing from the Lord.

God pairs—in marriages—and appoints all destinies.

The nations cannot exist or flourish without Israel in the midst of them. Israel cannot flourish unless God is in the midst of their families.

Man is bound to pay the same respect to his wife's father as he would to his own father.

A wife is like an altar, "like the altar in the temple; and she is even an atonement as the altar was."

"God has a seal and his seal is truth."

The Sanctuary of the Home

Observant Jews have been celebrating a home evening (Shabbat eve) as a religious ritual focused on the family ever since the institution of the Sabbath in the midst of wandering Israel. At its best the Jewish home is not a castle. It is a sanctuary. Much of Jewish worship is in the home. Passover is in the home. The rituals of circumcision and of the bar mitzvah take place in the home.

On Shabbat eve the mother lights the candles and embellishes the feast. The poorest man is enriched as he closes out the world and reaches toward God through the clustering of wife and children. Every song is a celebration of the Creation and the Creator. Every sip in the ritual process is symbolic of kinship in the family of God. The drawing in of strangers from beyond the family is to include them in the sense of belonging, of kinship, of family. The Sabbath disciplines of the law, some of them steep and demanding, are to make possible this level of joy.

From these teachings and rituals something is absent: the notion that the relation of the sexes is intrinsically evil. The Jews neither worship the body nor deny it. Marriage is recognized as one of the main things God wants men and women to do, a duty that is also the keenest of comforts. On Judgment Day, it is said, all of us will be asked, "Did you raise a family?" The single life—especially if it is deliberately chosen—is a misfortune, barrenness a source of anguish, and a good marriage the chief delight of a people who are sure God is good. Indeed the self-torturing view of life is countered by a famous Talmudic saying, "On the day of reckoning man will have to give account for every gift which his eyes beheld and which he did not enjoy."

If it is not a miracle it is at least remarkable that the Jews have survived, and survived with this element of their faith intact. Mighty cultures have sworn their annihilation, and both annihilation and assimilation have taken their toll. But the Jews live on. How has it happened? One fact is clear: Jews do not answer the question "Who am I?" except in terms of "Whose am I?" If there is sense in being "chosen," it includes being chosen both for suffering, and for blessedness as a family.

A first-century saying has it that "he who loves his wife as himself, and honors her more than himself; who leads his sons and daughters in the straight path, and marries them near their time of maturity—to his house the words of Job apply: 'Thou shalt know that thy tent is in peace.' " (Yebamoth 62b.) For the house of Abraham, that peace has always been in the midst of turmoil.

And in a way that no other nation can quite emulate, the inheritance and destiny of every Jew is bound up with that of every other. The family of Israel stands before God as one.

All these sayings from Judaism should be, as it were, on a theological pedigree chart, tracing back to original undistorted insight. But the history of Judaism lost touch, at least in its central stream, with the two ultimate recognitions that give meaning to the rest—the doctrine of the genuine pre-existence of man and the doctrine of a physical resurrection. Strangely, faith in God has not always been attended by faith in immortality and especially in the resurrected form. It remained for Joseph Smith not only to restore these doctrines but to restore the keys of authority and power to give them vitality and efficacy in our lives.

3

Jesus and the Family

Jesus was a Jew. The teachings of Jesus, the miracles of Jesus, the parables of Jesus are rooted in family consciousness. This fact has often been obscured and even repressed in traditional reading.

Marriage

For example, his first announcement of his role as the Anointed One was to a woman estranged. She was a prodigal daughter. And she was a Samaritan. The conversation occurred at Jacob's well—Jacob, the son and the father; Jacob who was to perpetuate the promises to Abraham and Isaac of a posterity "as the stars of heaven" (Exodus 32:13); Jacob, whose encounter with God, symbolized in a wrestling match with an angel, initiated for him as for us a new life and a new name: Israel; Jacob, whom we know from modern revelation is not a mere memory or a floating spirit but is resurrected and exalted with his companion to a familial throne forever (D&C 132:37).

What does Jesus teach the woman? He sits on the well (a gesture of identification?). He contrasts the water she draws from the well, which is only a temporary aid to thirst, with the living water he has to give. He says he himself is a well of living water which to those who receive him as Messiah will spring up into everlasting life. And how does she respond? "Sir, give me this water." And Jesus says, "Go, call thy husband, and come hither" (John 4:9-16).

The incident does not end there. But the point does—the Master was recognizing the proper family order.

Both in mortality and in modern revelation Jesus speaks of himself as the bridegroom. The modern Church is "as a bride adorned for that day when thou [the bridegroom] shalt unveil the heavens, and cause the mountains to flow down at thy presence, and the valleys to be exalted, the rough places made smooth; that thy glory may fill the earth." (D&C 109:74.) As he teaches he demonstrates that the bonds of the gospel are at their most powerful when they replicate the family relationship. His most frequent title for the Father is *Abba*. *Abba* is more intimate and less formal than the word *father*. It is closest to the endearing whisper of a little child—"Daddy."

Exactly the contrary conclusion is usually drawn from the passage that says, "Who is my mother? Who are my brethren?" It seems to define discipleship of Jesus as renunciation of such relationships. On the contrary, temporary disruptions occur when only "one of a family" accepts Christ. But discipleship leads eventually to reunion in the family sun. Spiritually Jesus becomes a begetting Father and tangibly we take on his likeness. This means we too are called to beget and nurture. The resounding promise of "a fullness and a continuation of the seeds"—the promise of everlasting procreation—then triumphs over all the forms of death that conspire against it. The worst tragedy—of our own making—is to be "severed from the ordinances of mine house" (D&C 121:19) and left "neither root nor branch" (D&C

133:64)—that is, with neither forbears nor posterity; stripped of our birthright and of our rebirth rites.

By modern revelation Jesus the Christ has revealed himself anew, and in these celestial principles he has given us the key whereby we may integrate his original sayings and acts. And thus it becomes clear that Jesus was true to his Jewish tradition, as in many of its strands the Jewish tradition was true to the foundation and the original dispensation of the gospel with Father Adam. There is no final doctrine of asceticism, nor of world-renouncing celibacy. There is no doctrine of solitary heavenly status. To be separate and single is to be less than fulfilled. The gospel of Jesus Christ affirms as its very crown and capstone the eternal perpetuation of marriage.

Miracles

Jesus' miracles are manifestations of compassion. But his most profound compassion emerges when a mortal disease or sin or encumbrance cuts across the unfolding family relationships. Jairus pleads in behalf of his daughter. A woman is without issue. Another woman suffers a continual kind of issue that prevents conception. The blind, the leprous, the deaf are all somebody's son, somebody's daughter, somebody's brother, and the plea for intervention for them is most often at their initiative. The cry that made Jesus weep in behalf of Lazarus comes from his two sisters, whose faith has been all but shattered. And it is to rejoice their hearts as well as to demonstrate his power over death that Jesus acts. It is never simply to isolate and insulate the individual that Jesus performs miracles. It is to put him in his place. The highest place is a secure link not only in the glorified family of the divine Father but in its earthly counterparts.

It should be added that Joseph Smith's revisions of troublesome passages also point in the same direction. For example: The account of the wedding feast at Cana seems in the King James Version to be an impudent condemnation of his own mother

("Woman, what have I to do with thee?"). The Joseph Smith Translation inverts that reading: "Woman, what wilt thou have me to do for thee? that will I do; for mine hour is not yet come" (John 2:4 JST). In both versions he proceeds to do as she asks. Here, and elsewhere, both in word and in act, motherhood is exalted. How could it be more exalted than in his cry from the cross: "Woman, behold thy son! [Disciple,] Behold thy mother"? (John 19:26, 27.)

Jesus' miracles are usually put into three categories: healings, exorcisms, and—as in the case of Lazarus—resuscitation. There is another way to classify them: They are mostly matters of life and death. He asks us to see him as a mother hen trying (and weeping when he fails) to gather her chicks. Wings provide warmth and protection. Jesus, like the sun, would arise "with healing in his wings." (The Book of Mormon adds he is a source of nourishment.) He says to the wondering multitude in the Americas: "How oft *have* I, how oft *would* I, how oft *will* I" gather you as "a hen gathereth her chickens under her wings, and have nourished you." (3 Nephi 10:4.)

In the category of providing for hunger and thirst are the water-into-wine miracle, the draught of fishes big enough to almost sink two ships, the feeding of the five thousand, the feeding of the four thousand. In the feedings of the multitudes, we are told, men, women and children gathered; they were done in a setting of families. After the Savior's resurrection there was the great haul of fishes. Like a genuine parent he prepares nourishment of every kind. In each case he provides more than enough, "enough and to spare." "I am come that they might have life, and that they might have it more abundantly."

The call to fruitfulness and the curse of barrenness show up in the incident of cursing the fig tree (whose leaves had advertised that it was producing when it was without a single fig). It was not filling the measure of its creation.

Healings include the nobleman's son: "Thy son liveth"; Peter's wife's mother healed; the only son of the widow of Nain raised; the daughter of Jairus (an only daughter) raised; the woman with the issue of blood healed (was she barren? and did she thereafter bear a child?).

Many of his healings include forgiveness, relieving men and women of the demon of guilt as well as of buffetings of evil possession.

All in all, the multitudes sought to touch him, for there went virtue out of him and healed those with faith (Luke 6:19). And they heard him gladly, for his words and his teachings could be taken home.

Parables

As for the parables, there are fifty-one of them, and they not only use familiar Jewish manners and customs of home life but they glorify them. Notice, again, how many parables have to do with living, growing, flourishing, and being fruitful: the children of the bridechamber, new wine in old bottles, the sower, the seed growing by itself, the wheat and tares, the mustard seed and the leaven, the lost sheep and the ninety and nine, the watchful servants, the good shepherd, the wedding feast, the great supper, the returning prodigal son, the servant and the master, the laborers in the vineyard, the two sons, the wicked husbandman, the king's son, the fig tree leaves, the ten virgins, the talents, the sheep and the goats. The undergirding theme: "Every plant, which my Heavenly Father has not planted, shall be rooted up" (Matthew 15:13).

All the "I am" metaphor statements say more than that Christ has access to the power of life. They *identify* him with life:

I *am* . . . the life.

I am the true vine (. . . ye are the branches).

I am the living bread which came down from heaven.

I am the living water.

I am the resurrection and the life.

I am the way, the truth, and the life.

4

Love

As I grope and grapple with the gospel program, I am thrown repeatedly against the questions: What is the real definition of love? Are there different kinds of love? What is the love the Lord our God commands without reservation? Here I can only sketch the deepest conclusions that emerge.

Said Joseph Smith:

> There is a love from God that should be exercised toward those of our faith, who walk uprightly, which is peculiar to itself, but it is without prejudice; it also gives scope to the mind, which enables us to conduct ourselves with greater liberality towards all that are not of our faith, than what they exercise towards one another. These principles approximate nearer to the mind of God, because it is like God, or Godlike. (*Teachings,* p. 147.)

This statement was not written in the aftermath of a moving and inspiring encounter with the Saints. It was written from a damp and depressing dungeon known as Liberty Jail after nearly four months there. Note that the love the Prophet writes of is *from*

God and is Godlike. And it is not just prejudicial. ("If ye love them which love you, what reward have ye? do not even the publicans the same.") It is not just birds of a feather flocking together, or honor among thieves. It is that peculiar kind of love that enables us to see beyond and feel beyond the personality clashes and irritations which so often spell ruin. But beyond that, the mind-expanding quality of this love extends to those who are not sympathetic to us, to those not of our faith.

Love, Light, and Law

Whatever else love is, it is a shining thing.

Some time ago a study group pursued every occurrence of the words *light* and *life* and *love* in the scriptures. One illuminating discovery was that all light is centered in God and the Son, for whom it is all but synonymous with the highest truth, good, beauty, and holiness. (See Truman G. Madsen, "Man Illumined," in *To the Glory of God*, Salt Lake City, Deseret Book, 1972, pp. 121-36.)

But all that was preface to another discovery: In the scriptures one of the opposites of love is darkness. The light that "fills the immensity of space" is a manifestation of love. Therefore, if the love of the Father does not "continue with us" (he does not withdraw it; we withdraw from it because of our insensitivity or rebellion), we "walk in darkness." If we would increase in love, it follows that we must increase in light. And if we would increase in light, the "light which groweth brighter and brighter until the perfect day," then, says modern revelation, we must, in the way of Christ, become "servants of all"—clearly, especially of those of our own household. Only thus may we become "possessors of all things" as promised, possessors of "the life and the light, the Spirit and the power, sent forth by the will of the Father through Jesus Christ, his Son. But no man is possessor of all things except he be purified and cleansed from all sin." (D&C 50:24, 26-28.)

Love Is Fire

In the spiritual as in the physical realm, light is intertwined with fire. In my *Four Essays on Love* it is written that "love is fire." Letters have come from around the world saying, "This is a mere metaphor. You are playing at poetry." Metaphor or not, the scriptures are full of it. And when their meaning is unpacked a cosmology emerges.

We are taught that "God dwells in everlasting burnings"; that even in "chaotic matter, which is element, . . . dwells all the glory" (*Teachings*, pp. 351-61); that "God, himself, will light up the world with his glory, making of it a body more brilliant than the sun that shines in yonder heavens" (Orson Pratt, *Journal of Discourses* 14:236); that "[the earth] will not then be an opaque body as it now is, but it will be like the stars of the firmament, full of light and glory; it will be a body of light" (Brigham Young, *Journal of Discourses* 7:163). "And when *it* shall be glorious, *we* shall be glorious also" (*Millennial Star,* vol. 12, p. 72).

Prophets ancient and modern choose the word *fire* to describe both the visual and the inward sensations of the glory of the Lord and of his Spirit. "The Spirit is like fire in our bones," they write. Says Nephi, "He hath filled me with his love [elsewhere "his power"] even unto the consuming of my flesh" (2 Nephi 4:21). Joseph Smith, in attempting to describe the pillar that descended to the Sacred Grove, first called it fire and then used the word *glory*. It seemed like fire but nothing was consumed. And it was not glaring nor hurtful as it both surrounded and enveloped him. "My soul was filled with love and for many days I could rejoice with great joy and the Lord was with me. . . ." (1832 account of the First Vision).

One kind of fire singes and withers and destroys. This kind hallows and nourishes and sanctifies. Baptism is of the Holy Ghost "and of fire" (3 Nephi 9:20; 12:1). The most powerful outpourings of the Holy Ghost have been described as "holy tongues of fire." Jesus "is like a refiner's fire." And we are promised that when he returns his presence "shall be as the melting fire that burneth, and as the fire which causeth the waters to boil" (D&C 133:41).

Since Einstein, physicists have been telling us that light may be understood both as a collection of particles and as a series of waves. That may well be true also of "light and life, spirit and power" that fill the immensity of space.

Love Is Self-Generating

While earthly light comes from expendable energy sources, the light that is love can increase without loss. If I give you a coin, a jewel, or a precious *objet d'art*, you have it and I do not. Your increase diminishes my possessions. But in the realm of the truer riches, my giving—of love—adds to rather than subtracts from the total sum of the universe. The more I give, the more I have. The more all of us are quickened by that love, the more there is to give and receive. For "intelligence cleaveth unto intelligence, . . . virtue loveth virtue, light cleaveth unto light" (D&C 88:40). And love begets love. The well cannot run dry.

Love Is Lawful

The concept that love is lawful counters the powerful illusion that love is free-floating and untrustworthy, that it comes and goes like the wind. Jesus instead teaches that the Spirit, which he once compared to wind (because we fail to recognize its origin), is the most constant thing in the universe. Mountains may disintegrate. It will not. It is the pure emanation of God and Jesus Christ; it endureth forever.

We are to pray for charity, for love, "with all the energy of heart," that we may be filled (Moroni 7:48). "Being filled" is more than a spasmodic impulse. The faithful may have a testimony that love need not "pass us by," provided only that we fulfill the conditions for its reception and for its transmission.

"I have fallen out of love," a man said recently, "and when love is dead it is really dead."

Said his stake president (who is also an authority on family studies), "You are out of love? Then you have stopped doing the things that generate love. You have lost touch with the source of love. Start over again."

"But I don't have the heart to do these things," the man replied.

"But you do. You have, if nothing else, the skeleton of an original covenant when you were in the full bloom of romantic love for your mate. If the flame has diminished, the spark has not. Fan it and you will find it increasing in your companion as in yourself."

Creation and Procreation

In our seminars Stephen Covey and I occasionally find sincere couples who have been led to believe that their physical union is justified if, and only if, they are seeking to bear children; that it has no other divinely approved purpose. We have occasionally asked "You feel this in the spirit of sacrifice?"

"Yes."

"You feel your lives can be truly unselfish only in your nurturing of your children?"

"Yes."

We have turned to one or the other, "Is your mate a child of God?"

"Yes."

"Don't you think your heavenly parents want him or her to be fulfilled? Don't you think your calling begins with him or her and then extends to your offspring?"

"We never thought of it that way."

Among the modern prophets there is unity that the purpose and power of union in marriage, if participated in with the right intent, is "honorable and sanctifying" and "develops the higher faculties and nobler traits of human nature, which the love-inspired companionship of a man and a woman alone can insure" (Joseph F. Smith). One of our leaders has written: "God is the author of conjugal love as he is of all other kinds of love." We are, of course, to multiply and replenish the earth. We are also to multiply and replenish each other in the "cultivation of those eternal principles of never-ending charity and benevolence, which are inspired by the Eternal Spirit" (Parley P. Pratt, *Key to the Science of Theology*, p. 164).

Such unions, modern revelation tells us, are "visited with blessings and not cursings" and are attended "with my power," saith the Lord, and are "without condemnation on earth and in heaven" (D&C 132:48).

Paul has brilliantly summarized how losing oneself in one's partner is also finding oneself. He writes (Joseph Smith Translation 1 Corinthians 7:4-5): "The wife hath not power of her own body, but the husband; and likewise also the husband hath not power of his own body, but the wife." Then he adds (in the JST), "Depart ye not one from the other, except it be with consent for a time, that ye may give yourselves to fasting and prayer; and come together again, that Satan tempt you not for your incontinency." (The King James version says, "Defraud ye not one the other.")

God Needs Our Love

In Western religious tradition a dominant theme is that God has no needs. He is portrayed as passionless, living in transcendent and static perfection. But Jesus clearly teaches otherwise. Everything he says and does assumes we can please or displease God, thwart him, even hurt him. He who is supposedly transcendent (even when the attempt is to identify him with Christ and speak of his "passion") cares for us. He is, therefore, vulnerable to our use of freedom.

Caring for someone magnifies one's capacities for pain. (In our self-protective moments that is why we shrink from lasting love—and settle for less. We would rather "not get involved.") If God truly cares for us perfectly—and that is the witness of those closest to him—his caring includes the anxiety of concern. He is not "above all that." He can be "touched with the feeling of our infirmities" (Hebrews 4:15), touched by the cry of our hearts. He can be touched in the sense that nothing matters more to him or to the Son, who paid the awful price of embodying his love, than our love. Finally, he can be touched in embrace, a royal embrace. It is no myth that we may one day be "encircled in the arms of his love" (D&C 6:20).

If this were not clear to Joseph Smith in his groping years as a boy, it came down on him clearly before his twenty-fifth year. As he translated a vision of Enoch he saw through his eyes that the Father, like the Son, can be troubled to tears in our indifference and hostility. When Enoch marveled and cried out (after naming many of the perfections of God), "O God, how is it *thou* canst weep?" the answer came: "Unto thy brethren I have said . . . that they should love one another, and that they should choose me, their Father; but behold, they are without affection, and they hate their own blood" (Moses 7:31, 33).

God the Father needs our love, as we need his. And he needs us to love those he loves. It is not blasphemy to affirm this. It is blasphemy to deny it. In his preface to the Doctrine and Covenants, he counsels that so long as everyone walks "in his own way, and after the image of his own God," so long as we "seek not the Lord to establish his righteousness," we shall be partakers of misery. "All will suffer until they obey Christ himself" (*Teachings*, p. 357).

5

Love at
Home

Stephen Covey and I have talked to couples, both alone and together, and sometimes to children, searching for common elements in stable and enduring relationships. We have compiled statistics which are striking in two ways: They show the dissatisfaction—the feeling that there is somehow more to be had, even much more, that the couple is missing. ("I feel gypped," one woman said.) At the other end they show that, even through terrible disillusion, there need not be dissolution of the marriage. And more impressive than the divorce and separation figures are the figures on how many in our society at large, and even more in the Church, try again.

Commitment the Key

One point is clear: There are no problemless marriages. And no one in this real world receives enough love, if "enough" means in word and act, feeling and fulfillment, day after day. But three common elements show up again and again among those who have endured "the burden and heat of the day":

1. A divinely-centered commitment that abides through disagreement, through pain and denial, and through adjustments and pressures.
2. Moments, however rare, when sharing is really sharing and the struggle seems infinitely worth it. (This can mean a sense of divine approval even while the partner or others of the family seem unappreciative or unresponsive.)
3. A willingness to take time and energy to make it work. This often means radical adjustments and long endurings.

The last point I wish to stress with three examples.

I know a couple "unequally yoked," both once-divorced. The wife had been a Latter-day Saint all her life. Her husband was religiously indifferent. She was educated and accomplished. He was competent, high-incomed. The marriage was tenuous.

After his conversion to the Church, and even after several years of service in it, he came to a stark realization: He had given his wife everything except himself. For the first time he recognized he was a loner, a self-centered man, placating his wife rather than cherishing her. He now resolved to put her at the heart of his very busy life, and began lingering in the little ways of sensitive affection—a note, a touch, a phone call. From that moment things changed. Their separation ended and a new life opened up. Now even their grown-up children can sense a tangible love between them.

I know another couple who were reasonably happy. Then a health problem arose that kept the man home in a long convalescence. The wife describes what happened:

"It used to be that if John occupied a chair in our home, he was either working with the checks at the beginning of the month, counseling or listening to someone who came to him for a special reason, eating, impatiently "wasting his time" watching a TV program I insisted he might enjoy (and this only momentarily), or sound asleep. Our moments of "communion" were so fleeting, and usually caught on the dead run, psychologically if not physically. The love we had for each other was felt and often expressed but seldom really enjoyed.

"However, since his illness, we have shared wonderful moments together. I have sat for hours by the side of his bed or chair, and there was no need for us to speak. The space between us was empty of words, and those were unnecessary. We have felt together a peace and companionship that cannot be sandwiched into a few quiet moments of frantically scheduled lives. I have seen John hold his little daughter for long periods of time in perfect peace and enjoyment. I have seen the child absorb her father's new kind of love and reciprocate in kind. All of our family relationships have taken on a new depth, because we have been able to share with each other not just more experiences but more understanding.

"What we have found together is too precious and personal and sacred to describe. Yet it is something all are entitled to. Why must we wait for such a crisis in order to find this kind of beauty? It seems we have to learn how important it is before we can make ourselves accept the conditions that will bring it into our lives."

A mother who was trying to teach "neurologically impaired" children was having success. But with one nine-year-old she perpetually failed. One night, driven to her knees, she asked over and over, "Why?" Her mind was led to formulate this answer: "You are saying, in effect, 'I love you, Rob, but I can't accept your actions.'" She understood that this was coming out as rejection of him.

The impression came clearly that she must say, "I love you, Rob, and I accept you as you are, actions and all." But she would have to *feel* what she was saying. She understood she already was saying all the right things and performing all the right actions. But there was lurking resentment in her heart for all the boy's disruptions. It was also given her that she must pray for this change of heart, that it would not come by will alone.

"To my joy I found I actually could accept Rob, actions and all. I suddenly realized how much more important he was than anything he was doing. On that day Rob began to change. He felt my love and basked in its warmth. He calmed down and became my most helpful student, always wanting to assist me. He was able to make real progress during the remaining three months of the class. I was overwhelmed by what I was witnessing. Everyone was amazed by his change. His parents came to see me and were thrilled by his improvement."

That teacher had now experienced the impact of unconditional love.

Unconditional Love

Hard-headed, thwarted, alienated parents and children may feel that unconditional love is a pious fraud. They see love and family loyalty at best to be frail and wavering things. Such love as is described and prescribed in this way seems unreachable. It is out of this world.

But that is just the point. The source of such love is far greater than anything in mortality. And that is why the Lord requires us to come to him in the sanctuary—in a most heavenly environment—to make unconditional covenants with Father and Son *before* we make unconditional covenants with each other as husband and wife.

Let me suggest four outcomes of Christlike love in the home.

First, you will have the joy of seeing another person become more and more a daughter or son of God. The eight-cow woman of the Johnny Lingo story became an eight-cow woman only when she learned that was how her man felt about her. It was his love, how much he cared, that created the beauty in her that no one else could see. It seems a sentimental notion that love is physically as well as spiritually transforming. But it is. Who has not seen how love for a face generates love *in* a face, and how a loving face becomes a lovable face, eliciting the very love it bestows?

Second, when you give love that way, even in the presence of bitterness and abuse—when you return a look full of daggers with a look full of love—eventually, if the partners are sensitive, one will want to give the same back. In the end such reciprocation, such a return wave, will enrich you. Over the long haul it is hard to be cared for and not care in return. The seeds will come to fruit —and the resulting bond will be greater than the sum of each person alone could have been. In these circumstances one plus one is far more than two.

But the converse is also true. Negative reciprocation will subtract from and weaken the bond. Nagging, pleading, "sending back the hurt I receive," denial, distance, playing hard to get, tricks and trades—these can help a marriage make "great strides backwards."

A third outcome is peace. Joseph Smith described some homes of his own time as places of "war, jangle, and contradiction." He said the truly illegitimate child is one who has hateful parents, who argue and are at variance with each other. Peace comes when you return no evil with evil, when you are kind in the presence of cruelty, when you are patient in the presence of impatience. This peace removes sadness and melancholy. And it removes the strongest self-deception (which is promoted by the adversary and increasingly sponsored in modern society): It is all someone else's fault.

Fourth is the "ripple effect." The parables keep seeping into our consciousness: the diminutive mustard seed becomes a tree where the birds may lodge, build their nests; a little candle lights up not just a square inch but a room, a home, a world, light enough for all; a city set on a hill cannot be hid. Jesus' own ministry, even after his charge "tell no man" (and without the advantages of modern television and satellite), was carried outward in ever-widening circles. Thus the one becomes a multitude, and one day may influence all.

Many of us have no long-range vision in much of our struggle. We think only of the moment—this time, this place, this circumstance. But think of ten generations of children who inherit such love. And their children. And theirs. Compared to this, empire-building is child's play. Personality-building is the work and the glory of the gods. Who can measure it? Anyone can count the seeds in an apple, but who can count the apples in a seed?

Just keeping one arm toward our forbears and one arm in the direction of our hoped-for posterity may turn out to be our mightiest contribution. In the end all the armies and military maneuvers, and all the so-called decisive battles, will have meant little. What matters in this perspective? What matter is what takes place in three temples: the temple, the home, and your own soul.

6

Tests of Circumstances

A young man and woman meet, fall in love, marry. How can the future appear anything but rosy? But along the way there will be a trial or two, in some cases severe ones. How will the couple or the individual meet such tests of circumstances?

Every so often one comes across a couple who dramatically demonstrate the power of spiritually rooted love against incredible odds. What is presented here is all firsthand from our "Love Finds a Way" file.

Example: Husband (seventy-eight) has Parkinson's disease with its ceaselsss tremor of arms and legs. Wife (two years younger) struggles with arthritis and insomnia. How do such seasoned mates cope? One way: At night, husband places hand under wife's neck while they lie in bed. Hand "automatically" massages and soothes. He prays for her through his mobile "laying on of hands." Wife is relieved, released to sleep. Husband then falls asleep. The shaking ceases.

Example: Couple bears four children, all normal. After two years the sons develop Hurler's syndrome. This is a reversing of all growth processes. Both become bedfast; one lives fifteen years, the other twenty-one. Each dies when there is not muscle enough left to breathe. In all those years the mother, keeping constant vigil, hardly leaves the house, and sometimes not even the room. Yet this home remains a neighborhood magnet; a healthy, wholesome, resilient place for family and visitors. And why? Because, in her words, through it all "my husband and I are still a stomach-grabbing pair of romantics." They are also (and therefore) Saints.

Example: Phone call comes to a temple president, "We wish to have our three adopted children sealed to us."

"That will be fine."

Arrangements are made. The next day the matron of the temple enters the nursery. Here are three radically affected Down's syndrome children. Each has been plucked from a different foundling home or hospital. "We were unable to have children," the couple explains. "We love them as our own."

Example: The wife and daughter of a recent convert are driving, rejoicing, when another car careens from the opposite lane into a head-on collision. Mother and daughter are killed. The other driver is thoroughly drunk in celebration of the birth of his first child. He walks away unscratched.

At home, in trauma and desolation, the bereaved husband after some days becomes aware that one person in the world is suffering more than he. He drives to the young man's home, knocks on the door, and confronts surprise and recoil with two quiet sentences: "Do not be afraid. I have come to tell you I forgive you."

Example: Wheelchaired spastics meet, fall in love, and are married in the temple. Years later husband phones bishop: "I took Mary to the hospital to have surgery for a tumor. They delivered a seven-pound eight-ounce boy." The child is normal.

Example: Wife of a General Authority suffers stroke and extensive paralysis. For five years she is confined to bed. In the last year she is unable to speak. Husband moves her bed into the living room and surrounds her with bustling life, speaking to her in all their accumulated inside jokes and code phrases and love pats. She can only reply with her eyes. They are full of peace. Visitors say, "How can one think evil of a gospel which has created a face like that?"

Example: A dedicated nun is converted—first, to the holiness of marriage; second, to the vitality of the restored gospel of Jesus Christ; third, to the proposal of a Latter-day Saint widower. After some years of "senior citizen" marriage she bears her testimony, saying, among other things, "I love his first wife as I love him."

Example: Renowned sociologist retires at sixty-five. At home he and his wife hold long discussions: "What is the greatest contribution we can make in our remaining years?" At length they are as one in the decision: to raise, in love, a child in the patterns of Christ.

Adoption agencies are brutal in ridicule. "At your age? No way!" After twenty-six official refusals, fasting and prayer, much patience, and infinite red tape, they are permitted to adopt (first time in America) an orphan boy from the Far East. They fill up his life and he fills up theirs.

Example: Six-year-old daughter ventures into neighbor's yard and darts, on her blind side, into man and rotary lawnmower. Later her parents stand over her in the intensive care unit trying to decide how to tell her that her foot is amputated. She feels their anxiety, reads the message, and says, "It's all right, mother. I won't need two feet to love my children, only two arms."

Example: Sister Zina follows Sister Eliza from a meeting of sobering admonition. "Sister So-and-so sent me to tell you that she doesn't love you any more." "But," Eliza replies, "I love her. Nothing she can say or do can change that."

Example: Wife says—to the acid comment of a young lady who calls her a "Church widow"—"I could not love my husband if I did not know his soul is as broad as eternity."

Example: Lady missionary comes from a broken home, serves in the mission field, returns home in fear that she will be like her alcoholic mother. Marriage prospects fade. She is counseled, "If you need a friend, be a friend. If you cannot channel your affectionate gifts in marriage, channel them in service." She discovers a talent within herself for communicating with retarded children. Long years later she finds that others have discovered in her a more lovable person, including a man who wants to become her husband.

Example: Hemophiliac in braces is called on a mission. His president does not "mollycoddle" him but presses him to the limits of faith and determination. He serves well and becomes rooted in the scriptures. He marries in the faith that his pain and his problem (which eventually requires 3,200 blood transfusions) will not be visited on his children. It isn't. The marriage survives as partners almost reverse roles: wife is breadwinner in a hard, competitive role outside the home, husband hobbles through much of the housekeeping and "works" only one week in three, keeping shop and business going via telephone. Their home is a haven. The children grow up with unusual "bonds" of love.

Example: Woman in mid-thirties is paralyzed from the waist down. Husband, already unfaithful, hopes for her death. Long therapy and great faith enable her to function again. Then husband abandons her. Confined to a wheelchair she raises her children single and single-handedly and finds her niche in the Church as a youth leader, a writer, and an expert in physical rehabilitation. The absence of priesthood in her home is, in a measure, made up by solicitous assigned brethren in the ward and stake. Not a trace of bitterness shows in her face.

Example: Daughter, born to prominent parents, witnesses a series of horrendous trangressions followed by excommunication. Her first response is bitter hate and a rejection of all the parents represent, including the gospel. Then, as she comes to view the wreckage of other wrecked families, she asks for a leadership role among singles. She becomes a great matchmaker, reconstructing broken hearts and strengthening feeble knees. Thus far no match has been made with her. She continues to serve.

"The highest type of discernment is that which perceives in others and uncovers for them their better natures, the good inherent with them" (Elder Stephen L Richards, *Conference Report*, April 1950, p. 163).

Finding Meaning in Suffering

Hugh Hibley uncovered the following apocryphal quotation. If it is not an authentic echo of the words of Christ, it is anyway a profound insight: "If you knew how to suffer you would be able not to suffer. Learn how to suffer and you should be able not to suffer." (*New Testament Apocrypha*, Hennecke & Schneemelcher, 2:230, lines 31-42.)

A renowned center for patients with chronic pain is headed by a recent convert to the Church. He is a neurosurgeon. Pharmacologists, psychiatrists, psychologists, all combine with him as a "pain team" to help patients cope with unremitting pain. Commenting on a line in one of my essays—"In us and in others, love is the Lord's preventive medicine; and, as we are now learning, it is the only lasting foundation for powerful therapy, whether for sin or for suffering" (Truman G. Madsen, *Four Essays on Love*, Bookcraft, 1977, p. 15)—he concludes: "We have found that unless there is a 'significant other' in the life of the sufferer—at least one person who cares about him and about whom he cares—all our efforts to diminish or relieve the pain are weak. On the other hand, if there *is* a significant other, a person who cares, the sufferer is much better able to endure and overcome."

We should know this from the New Testament and from our own history. Saintly men and women from the beginning of this dispensation demonstrate that love can soothe the most difficult and tragic hours. It is an ancient tradition that the same Hebrew letters that mean anguish *(tzarah)* also spell another word which means light *(tzohar)*.

It is the calling of the faithful to find the light of meaning in suffering. It is not just absurd, pointless, mindless. Our sufferings can, through Christ, be turned to good. We can generate light out of darkness and glory out of anguish, and end not with bitterness but with compassion.

"Men have to suffer," taught the Prophet Joseph Smith, "that they may come upon Mount Zion and be exalted above the heavens" (*Teachings*, p. 323). That is what it means to be Christlike. There are, apparently, no celestial personalities except those who have known affliction—known it by experience. This does not mean that we seek pain. It means that we bear the pains that our life-missions and our family responsibilities require us to bear.

When we find the Lord, we can rejoice in the midst of affliction which is swallowed up in Christ. We may one day say with Brigham Young, "I never felt the peace and power of the Almighty more copiously poured upon me than in the keenest part of our trials. They appeared nothing to me." (*Journal of Discourses*, 1:313.)

The feeling "I want out" is often accompanied by a feeling "I am being held back." Studies of just such strained circumstances in a variety of homes have led one scientific group to the same conclusion as that of the gospel: Our most vital growth often occurs when we are in crisis. Again and again I have heard testimonies from thoughtful, seasoned, and (if I may say so) battle-scarred partners who say, without rancor, "My trial has turned out to be my blessing." They see the distinction between freedom from and freedom for.

We spend tremendous energy defending our rights to freedom from—from interference, from cumbersome red tape, from rules and regulations, from threats, from oppressive acts. All that leaves out of account freedom *for*—freedom for becoming what we have it within us to become. One can have precious little freedom from and great freedom for. Some of Joseph Smith's most productive months of soul growth and kinship with Christ came while he was bound up and burdened in a small jail in Liberty, Missouri.

Of course, it is not easy. Of course, we shrink. Of course, we cry out as did Joseph, "How long, O Lord?" To him as to us the Lord replies, "If thou endure it well . . . thine afflictions shall be but a small moment; And . . . God shall exalt thee on high." (D&C 121:7-8.)

Burning in Gratitude

The cumulative wisdom (there is a ream of it in our files) is that, as one sister sums it up, "I never knew a thoroughly depressed person who was counting his blessings." She had room to talk. She was a nonmurmurer who had been paralyzed from the waist down for thirty-five years.

"Tell us about your trials," visitors would say.

"No," she would reply, "but I'll tell you about my blessings."

Dwelling on what one owes in honest gratitude is one of the Lord's most mighty therapies against depression, despair, and turning in on oneself.

Often I have put to classes the question: "In modern revelation two commandments are added to the Decalogue. What are they?"

Silence.

"These commandments were handed down to us with the same authority and power as those at Sinai," I say, to challenge them. "What are they?"

No hands.

The answer is in section 59 of the Doctrine and Covenants, our great Sabbath-observance revelation. It was given to a cluster of harassed converts who had arrived in Zion with only a faint idea of what Zion could be. The commandments:

1. Thou shalt thank the Lord thy God in all things.
2. Thou shalt offer a sacrifice unto the Lord thy God in righteousness, even that of a broken heart and a contrite spirit. (D&C 59:7,8.)

The Lord commands gratitude? The Lord commands contrition? Yes, with a promise. "He who receiveth all things with thankfulness shall be made glorious; and the things of this earth shall be added unto him, even an hundred fold, yea, more." (D&C 78:19.)

"How can I thank God? Everything in my life is a shambles."

The evidence is that ingratitude is as damaging to our personalities as it is a permeating plague on marriage and family life. It is a species of selfishness. It is also a symptom of repressed vision. For it deliberately "refuses to count" what has been given, granted, as well as borne and foreborne by the Lord Jesus Christ and by those around us.

In contrast (it is alleged that the Prophet Joseph Smith taught), if we would kneel daily and present before the Lord, and in the presence of our companion, a heart's inventory of blessing, if we would feel before we thank, and thank before we ask, we would find ourselves among the radiant ones. For gratitude compounds in expression with blessings, even those we think of as the minimal blessings, the small mercies of life. Gratitude—remembering the positive—can remain alive and well even in the midst of serious setbacks and failures. It preserves family love.

Notice also that the promises attendant on a "glad heart and a cheerful countenance" are both temporal and spiritual. "The fullness of the earth is yours"—houses, barns, orchards, gardens, vineyards, things to please the eye and gladden the heart, things to strengthen the body as well as enliven the soul, things for taste and for smell (D&C 59). All these are of the nature of celestial life. And "we may even here begin to enjoy that which shall be in full hereafter" (Teachings, p. 296).

7

Temple
and Home

In the century and a half since the dedication of the Kirtland Temple, a profound heritage of temple consciousness has grown in our midst. We all wish to drink more deeply of the fountain. We are counseled over and over that this depends upon us, upon our own spiritual preparation, our own probing and pondering and praying. No one presumes to be our teacher. We are taught to seek divine teaching. Joseph Smith said: "The best way to obtain truth and wisdom is not to ask it from books, but to go to God in prayer, and obtain divine teaching." (*Teachings*, p. 191.)

Ten Purposes of the Temple

Yet in searching the counsels of our leaders, Stephen Covey and I have distilled ten concrete assurances concerning the meaning of temple worship which can give our quest some focus.

1. The temple is a "conservator of the great truths of the gospel" (John A. Widtsoe, *A Rational Theology*, p. 127). It is so packed, so freighted with the riches of celestial truth, that "only a fool" would attempt to unravel it into prosaic restatement. "We

live in a world of symbols. No man or woman can come out of the temple endowed as he should be, unless he has seen, beyond the symbols, the mighty realities for which the symbols stand." (*A Rational Theology*, p. 62.) It is a "house of learning" (D&C 109:8) where we may be taught not only the vital truths of life in the setting of eternal life, but those "hidden treasures" (D&C 89:19) which are reserved for the faithful, and which, as President Harold B. Lee testified, can be known powerfully in the heart as well as the head. From the beginning the Prophet taught that all these temple insights are "always governed by the principle of revelation" (*History of the Church* 5:2); but also that even "the weakest of the Saints" may receive them "as soon as they are prepared." What can emerge is wisdom—knowledge applied to decision.

2. The temple is a kind of observatory, as Hugh Nibley has written; built "four square by the compass," a place designed for us "to get our bearings" on the universe and our own lives. Elder George F. Richards spoke of the temple as "a measuring rod" by which we may over and over find our way through the struggles and confusions of our mortal journey and our individual missions (see *Utah Genealogical and Historical Magazine*, vol. 19, p. 149).

3. The temple is a house of prayer, of fasting and prayer; and for "the offering up of your most holy desires unto me" (D&C 95:16). It is therefore a place to bring our family perplexities and needs. Like the malignant demon of which Christ spoke as he descended from the mount, some of our weak and sinful habits may be the kind that can only be overcome through prayer and fasting." (See James E. Talmage, *Jesus the Christ*, p. 385.) Says Elder John A. Widtsoe, "I would rather go there [the temple] to solve the problems that afflict me in life than anywhere else" (*Utah Genealogical and Historical Magazine*, vol. 21, p. 97), and this view was shared by his wife. Elder Melvin J. Ballard adds, "When in the sacred walls of these buildings, while you are entitled to the Spirit of the Lord, and in the silent moments, the

answer will come" (*Utah Genealogical and Historical Magazine,* vol. 23, p. 147).

4. Temples are places of covenant and promise, out of which come discernment, sensitizing us to true and false influences. The Lord refers to a temple as a sanctuary where he may "endow [us] with power from on high" (D&C 38:32; 95:8; 105:11, 33; 109:35). Thus, "our temples give us power, a power based on enlarged knowledge and intelligence, a power from on high, of a quality with God's own power" (Elder John A. Widtsoe, *Utah Genealogical and Historical Magazine,* April 1921, p. 63). We are to receive these blessings, Joseph Smith taught, "in order that you may be prepared and able to overcome all things" (*Teachings,* p. 91). Our covenants are, as President Harold B. Lee writes, "an embodiment or of unfolding of the covenants each person should have assumed at baptism." (*Youth and the Church,* Deseret Book, p. 143). They are "calculated to unite our hearts, that we may be one in feeling and sentiment" (*Teachings,* p. 91). By union of feeling we obtain power with the heavens. The covenants confer upon us the "armor of God," a protection which, writes Joseph Fielding Smith, "the man who does not go to the temple does not have" (*Utah Genealogical and Historical Magazine,* vol. 21, p. 97). Thus the temple is a fortress—there we withdraw from the world in order to return fortified to the struggle.

5. Temples are places of nourishment. From the days of the ancient temple of Solomon, sacred tradition teaches, the temple is, or is built upon, the very "navel of the universe," our link with all creative powers. Joseph was commanded to pray at Kirtland that through the temple we might "grow up in thee, and receive a fulness of the Holy Ghost, and be organized according to thy laws [celestial laws], and be prepared to obtain every needful thing" (D&C 109:15). Our "growing up" involves nurture in the surroundings of the divine life. It centers in him who *is* the Life. He has promised, "I will manifest myself to my people in mercy in this house" (D&C 110:7). "Most of all things," wrote Elder

Franklin D. Richards, "I desire the Holy Spirit which giveth light, yea, life more abundantly of both body and spirit." (See *Improvement Era*, vol. 54, p. 168.) This enlivening power, which we are commanded to seek with our whole souls, not only gives us flashes of pure intelligence to meet our strains; it "quickens" us so that we live on a new level, a new ocean, as it were.

6. The temple is "the house of the Lord." All the pure in heart who come into it shall see God.

> It is a great promise that to the temples God will come, and that in them man shall see God. What does this promised communion mean? Does it mean that once in a while God may come into the temples, and that once in a while the pure in heart may see God there; or does it mean the larger thing that the pure in heart who go into the temples, may there, by the Spirit of God, always have a wonderfully rich communion with God? I think that is what it means to me and to you and to most of us. We have gone into these holy houses, with our minds freed from the ordinary earthly cares, and have literally felt the presence of God. In this way, the temples are always places where God manifests himself to man and increases his intelligence. A temple is a place of revelation. (John A. Widtsoe, "Temple Worship," *Utah Genealogical and Historical Magazine*, vol. 12, p. 56.)

7. Temples are, as Elder Joseph Fielding Smith has written, "places of sanctification" (see *Improvement Era*, vol. 54, p. 798). The presence of and ordination to the priesthood and ultimately the fulness of the priesthood are there. ("Go to and finish the temple, and God will fill it with power, and you will then receive more knowledge concerning this priesthood" (*Teachings*, p. 323). To receive knowledge of the priesthood is one thing. To receive the priesthood itself is another. Both are a privilege of the temple. As we "magnify our callings—which are epitomized in the home—then, according to promise, we are "sanctified by the Spirit unto the renewing of [our] bodies" (D&C 84:33). Perhaps this is the meaning of Elder John A. Widtsoe's statement that "no other church requirement lifts man to a nearer likeness of the Lord" (*Gospel Interpretations*, Bookcraft, 1947, p. 103).

8. "The endowment," Joseph Smith taught, "was to prepare the disciples for their missions in the world" (*Teachings*, p. 274). At Kirtland he prayed that "from this place they may bear exceedingly great and glorious tidings in truth, unto the ends of the earth." We think of this as extending the message of the gospel in missionary roles. That clearly includes teaching at home. We should carry the spirit of the temple into our homes to qualify, intensify, and liven our efforts to grasp teaching moments with our children and with each other. It is a place where we are to be "instructed more perfectly" in order that we may instruct more perfectly (see D&C 97: 13, 14) "in theory, in principle, and in doctrine."

9. The temple is described as a "place of thanksgiving" (D&C 97:13), a place of "memorials" (D&C 124:39). It is the proper place to "give thanks unto God in the Spirit for whatsoever blessing ye are blessed with" (D&C 46:32). It is the place where "I may reveal my ordinances." In revealing his ordinances, the Lord is revealing things "which have been kept hid from before the foundation of the world" (D&C 124:40, 41). "If thou shalt ask, thou shalt receive revelation upon revelation, knowledge upon knowledge, that thou mayst know the mysteries and peaceable things—that which bringeth joy, that which bringeth life eternal" (D&C 42:61).

10. Finally, the temple is a place of the unifying of all ordinances through firsthand participation. "Reading the experience of others, . . ." Joseph Smith said, "can never give *us* a comprehensive view of our condition and true relation to God. Knowledge of these things can only be obtained by *experience through the ordinances of God set forth for that purpose*." (*Teachings*, p. 324; italics added.) Experience is always more than abstract or conceptual understanding. Through it we can have the very law and power of God written into our flesh, into our "inward parts," our very limbs and tissues. Jesus promised anciently, and again in modern revelation (D&C 88:67), that if our eyes are single to his glory our whole bodies shall be filled with light. (An ancient

tradition says that there was a time when the whole body could think. We are promised a time to come when the righteous shall comprehend all things [see D&C 88:67].) The Prophet Joseph summarized the process: "Being born again, comes by the Spirit of God through ordinances" (Teachings, p. 162). Soul-consuming rebirth comes through the higher ordinances of the temple, which are the reenactment and the dramatic rehearsal of all ordinances of the kingdom of God.

We think, or tend to think, of these as stages through which we pass once and "once and for all." Clearly it is intended that the pattern and order of the house of God is repetitive. There is need for continual participation. Prophets teach that we are only beginning, that we now have only the sign and shadow, as it were, of an eternal order to be opened to us more fully hereafter. "The order of the house of God," the Prophet Joseph said, "has been, and ever will be, the same, even after Christ comes; and after the termination of the thousand years it will be the same; and we shall finally enter into the celestial kingdom of God, and enjoy it forever." Our present temple experiences are "a prelude of those joys that God will pour out on that day" when we inherit the fullness. (Teachings, p. 91.)

Our history, like our doctrine, is full of testimony that a temple sacrificially built and faithfully dedicated will bring down the Lord's glory. "My glory shall rest upon it" (D&C 97:15).

When the question is raised—"Why be married in the temple? Why not just elope?" we often say in essence, "Because only temple marriages are forever." But that puts all the emphasis on extent and duration. It says nothing of the quality and power and intensity of the love which can alone justify such duration. So let us rather say, "Because only in the temple are you placed in covenant-harmony with divine powers which will eventually so infuse and fuse your love that it will be *worth* perpetuating for-ever."

We are sometimes challenged, "You mean I cannot love my wife or my husband or children fully without some conferral in the temple?"

Our answer: "Exactly."

"You mean that what I am now feeling isn't love?"

"It is the beginning of real love. But a marriage will not last forever based on what you feel now. You must both receive and give an ever-richer quality of love. The keys and glory of that love are in the sanctuary where Jesus Christ is present from beginning to end. You cannot begin nor continue with each other except with him."

Dedicated Homes

President Harold B. Lee once asked, "If a couple is not yet prepared to be married in the temple, where should they be married?"

His hearers guessed: in the local chapel? in a sequestered cultural hall? in a hall of justice?

"No," Elder Lee replied, "in the home. Next to the temple, the home is the most sacred place on earth."

This insight quickened the first generation of Saints. After cleaning and ordering their homes, even their hovels, they held a dedicatory service. It was like a fresh beginning, consecrating dwelling and family to holy purposes and cleansing the dwelling of the lingering influences of earlier, perhaps desecrating, inhabitants. With faith and confidence they invoked the priesthood. Patriarchal and matriarchal rights of the parents were embodied in a dedicatory prayer. The act was also a symbol of consecration of ownership now transferred, in spirit at least, to the Lord. The Prophet Joseph Smith himself gathered his family together and went through this process in their modest log cabin in Nauvoo.

Our present leaders counsel couples in the sanctuary that their homes are to become mini-temples. "Even if you have to live in a tent in a vacant lot," President Spencer W. Kimball said, "look upon your home as a sanctuary." (One couple I know remove their shoes before entering their own room.) And the Lord's description of the temple at Kirtland may be applied point for point to the home: "a house of prayer, a house of fasting, a house of faith, a house of learning, a house of glory, a house of order, a house of God" (D&C 88:119). Also a house of worship (D&C 109:14).

But how can this be, we may respond, when a home is a place of hard, manual, sweaty work; a place of fun and hilarity; and a place whereby "all things pertaining to an inferior kingdom" are dumped into our midst via a Urim and Thummim called television? It can be. It can surround all of life. "All things unto me are spiritual," the Lord said (D&C 29:34). But the home is, and remains, a sanctuary only to the degree that the persons within it are consecrated. Then, for all of the mixture of laughter and tears, struggle, conflict, and growing pains, there is a tangible difference. People who enter such a home are "constrained to acknowledge" that it is a place where the Lord's Spirit is recognizable. And all who come, family as well as strangers, are heartened in that atmosphere. We observe that spirit emanating from single-parent homes too.

Whether parents go through formal dedicatory ceremonies or not, that Spirit should follow our visits to the temple and our expansions of understanding in the gospel that they evoke. The Millennium will come, Elder George Q. Cannon once observed, only when such homes dot the landscape. Eventually they will be a far-flung community, a world-neighborhood which by its very existence removes the curse of blight and leavens the human family with peace.

President Hugh B. Brown sums it up:

> Celestial marriage enables worthy parents to perform a transcendently beautiful and *vital service as priest and priestess in the temple of the home.* This training will help to prepare them for the exalted position of king and queen in the world to come, where they may reign over their posterity in an ever-expanding kingdom. (*You and Your Marriage,* Salt Lake City, Bookcraft, 1960, p. 193; italics added.)

Man and Woman as Redeemers

A contemporary writer observes: "For love to be fulfilling to woman, she must be able to look upon her lover as a redeemer, that is, as an individual who, in the role of God, transforms her in order to make ultimate fulfillment possible for her.'' (Peter Koestenbaum, *Religion in the Tradition of the Phenomenology,* D. Van Nostrand Co., Inc., Princeton, N.J., 1967.) ''This is impossible,'' the author concludes, ''or at best rare.''

Recognizing that the statement falls short of the gospel vision, if it were not impossible, what could make it possible?

1. The man and the woman must have inherited or received supernatural gifts. Otherwise, talk of assuming the ''role of God'' is terrible presumption.

2. In giving and receiving, both man and woman must be acting in a way that authoritatively represents the Divine. They would need to be equipped with divine authority, with the Holy Priesthood.

3. Their relationship to each other could not be just linear but must be triangular. They could reach each other only if they both were centered in God. That would require a covenant, a new covenant, an everlasting covenant, made with God first and then with each other. And that double fidelity —a fidelity to God and to each other—if violated, would mean a withdrawal of ''transforming power.''

4. If their union aspired to be ''in the imitation of God,'' that could only be achieved if the ultimate truth about God is that he is perfected in priesthood and parenthood, as the essence of godhood—and that creation and procreation are not mere mortal projections of a fallen world. Instead eternal life is the union of eternal lives. Salvation is never individual but always dual. But then, as President Hugh B. Brown has said, ''Marriage is and should be a sacrament'' (*You and Your Marriage,* Bookcraft, 1960, p. 13), the highest sacrament, the supreme fulfillment of saintliness.

Our temples make possible for us all four of these conditions.

Over the years we have gathered statements from all of the modern prophets, beginning with Joseph Smith, under the label ''to the righteous but unmarried.'' They uniformly promise that "no good thing" will be withheld from those who are without companions. They counsel against letting discouragement or impatience lead to compromise or a "settle-for-less" submission to an unbelieving wife or husband. "All in due time." "All in due time."

8

Church and Family Callings

Many a man and woman has aspired to office and calling in the Church. Sometimes they feel "passed over," "left to themselves." With some exaggeration they say they are left to the depressing tasks of "dishes, diapers, and drudgery." Without betraying experiences too intimate and too sacred, we can report that many such persons have come alive to the nature of true greatness:

Hear President Lorenzo Snow:

> The glorious opportunity of becoming truly great belongs to every faithful elder in Israel; it is his by right divine, and he will not have to come before this [the Twelve] or any other quorum to have his status defined. He may be a god in eternity; he may become like his Father, doing works which his Father did before him, and he cannot be deprived of the opportunity of reaching this exalted state. ("Characteristic Sayings of Lorenzo Snow," March 9, 1922, p. 209.)

This truth which came to Lorenzo Snow with power ("Nothing was ever revealed more distinctly than that was to me") was confirmed when he sat with the multitudes in the grove in Nauvoo and listened to the Prophet Joseph Smith's climactic King Follett discourse. The "great secret" is that we are, in fact, procreated in the image and likeness of God and therefore are embryonic gods. Lorenzo drew from it two conclusions which we sometimes fail to draw. First:

> I never sought to be a seventy or high priest, because this eternal principle was revealed to me long before I was ordained to the priesthood. The position which I now occupy [he was President of the Church] is nothing compared to what I expect to occupy in the future. (Special Collections, Brigham Young University.)

We may think it an achievement to hold high office, to sit on the stand, to wear the badge of official Churchwide recognition, but that is a temporary office in a temporary organization. Our destiny is not so fragile. The family does not exist to glorify the Church. It is precisely the reverse: the Church is the instrument for the glorification of the family. The priesthood itself and all of its opportunities for service in the wider Church family culminates in a patriarchal priesthood, a fatherly priesthood. This priesthood, in its fullness, leads to glories compared with which any role in the present Church launching pad fades into final insignificance. Family exaltation transcends them as the airplane transcends the bumblebee.

Second, Lorenzo Snow said: "This thought in the breasts of men filled with the light of the Holy Spirit, tends to purify them and cleanse them from every ambitious or improper feeling." (Special Collections, Brigham Young University.)

Family exaltation is not, as one perceptive non-Mormon writer has said, "a führer-principle," not a quest for dictatorial power or coercion. It is not, in the words of Elder Charles W. Penrose, "man's attempt to dethrone God." It is God's gloriously unselfish attempt to exalt man into His full likeness—sharing all that He has and all that He is; and sharing the burden, the burden of the whole eternal family to serve each other in order to bring forth love.

Brigham Young said:

We are created for the express purpose of increase. There are none, correctly organized, but can increase from birth to old age. What is there that is not ordained after an eternal law of existence? It is the Deity within us that causes increase. Does this idea startle you? Are you ready to exclaim, "What! The Supreme in us!" Yes, he is in every person upon the face of the earth. The elements that every individual is made of and lives in, possess the Godhead. This you cannot now understand, but you will hereafter. The Deity within us is the great principle that causes us to increase, and to grow in grace and truth. (*Journal of Discourses*, 1:93.)

The Exalted Woman

Elsewhere we have summarized the redemptive understandings of woman that are implicit and explicit in the doctrines, ordinances, and patterns of the restored church. (See "Woman, What Have I to Do with Thee?", Ricks College Devotional, February 1, 1977.) Here we cite Elder James E. Talmage on the eventual oneness of those who fill the measure of their creation:

In the restored church of Jesus Christ, the Holy Priesthood is conferred, as an individual bestowal, upon men only, and this in accordance with the divine requirement. It is not given to woman to exercise the authority of the Priesthood independently; nevertheless, in the sacred endowments associated with the ordinances pertaining to the house of the Lord, woman shares with man the blessings of the Priesthood. When the frailties and imperfections of mortality are left behind, in the glorified state of the blessed hereafter, husband and wife will administer in their respective stations, seeing and understanding alike, and co-operating to the full in the government in their family kingdom. Then shall woman be recompensed in rich measure for all the injustice that womanhood has endured in mortality. Then shall woman reign by Divine right, a queen in the resplendent realm of her glorified state, even as exalted man shall stand, priest and king unto the Most High God. Mortal eye cannot see nor mind comprehend the beauty, glory, and majesty of a righteous woman made perfect in the celestial kingdom of God. ("The Eternity of Sex," *Young Woman's Journal*, vol. 25, p. 602.)

*. . . there are no heights to which man shall aspire and obtain in which
woman shall not be, side by side, with him."* (Melvin J. Ballard, cited in
You and Your Marriage, p. 159.)

Recently, a man dragged his wife into a stake president's
office, thrust her in a chair, and said, "Now, president, you tell
my wife to obey my priesthood. Then all our problems at home
will be solved."

The president opened his Doctrine and Covenants to section
121, looked into the man's eyes, and said quietly, "According to
what I read here, you have no priesthood." (See vss. 36-37.)

President Spencer W. Kimball reiterated that the word *rule*, in
the sense of "thy husband . . . shall rule over thee" (Genesis
3:16), is not to be read *dominate* or *force*. It should be translated
preside. Indeed, it was his grandfather, Heber C. Kimball, long
before the exploitation of women had become a political issue,
who said that "no woman can be saved who is ruled by a man,
and vice versa." We are to be ruled by only one: God. And he
rules in the power and in the manner of the priesthood—that is,
in a long-suffering, universal sharing of both privilege and
accountability.

Husbands and wives are each other's counselors. Decisions
made in unity are promised greater strength and divine sanction
than others. "Be agreed as touching all things ye shall ask," is the
modern admonition. Conduct of marriage and the government of
the home, we believe, is rooted in the same principles and in
common consent. All members of the family are to have "input."
The question should not just be "What do you think about it?"
but "How do you feel about it?" The advantage of Stephen
Covey's "win/win" approach (see chapter 25) is simply this: It
works! We observe that in the home (and even in efficiency-
minded organizations) the concern to "get through an agenda,"
to stick to the "rational" and "factual" analysis without exchange of honest personal feelings, is in the end not more but less
effective.

"Husbands, love your wives, even as Christ also loved the church, and gave himself for it" (Ephesians 5:25). But "giving oneself" is often the reverse of the world's definition of power. So be it. The Master said of himself, "My power lieth beneath" (D&C 63:59). Sooner or later our covenants to love our companions will include the requirement to serve, to sacrifice.

But if this is said to alert men—husbands, fathers—about the corruptions of power, the same goes for the woman. Power struggles can corrode a woman as they can a man, can distort her own ministrations in the family, in the relationship with her husband, and in the world. The powers of heaven are available to her only when she, too, seeks to replace coercion with persuasion, impatience with long-suffering, harsh words with gentle ones, haughty judgment with gracious meekness, and pretended manipulative "love" with the genuine article—love unfeigned. These fruits of the Spirit enlarge the soul. Their counterparts shrink and shrivel it.

The miracle—and it is the most staggering one in the kingdom —is that there are such people, there is such behavior, all around us. There are such changes—from temper tantrums to mellowness, from prideful power grabs to genuine sharing. And when Lorenzo Snow observed one such glorious woman, who put it all together in the midst of the daily grind, he exclaimed, "A mother who has brought up a family of faithful children ought to be saved if she never does another thing!" ("Characteristic Sayings of Lorenzo Snow.")

Gathering Honey

Among psychologists there is disagreement on whether love flourishes most with "togetherness" or with "apartness." The gospel teaches that there are times for intensive care and times for deliberate distance; times for almost suffocating closeness and times when love is best nourished at departings and individual private paths; times for soul-felt sharing, and times for rejuvenating solitude.

A marriage that does not have some balance in these is a marriage that will sooner or later be in trouble. When a wife or husband must leave the home to answer calls that are commissioned and proper for the Church or for the community, how does the companion view it? As loss? As the interruption or sacrifice of their relationship? Or as the *preparation of its enhancement?* Surely if a partner is blessed and benefited in the experience of other contacts or is lighted up in the Lord's work, he/she comes home at a level better able to share with and to focus on the other.

I know men and women who have "resisted release" from Church callings because, as they confide, "When I come home from prayer meetings and councils and assignments I bring a spirit I have received there that otherwise is often missing. And my companion responds in kind." "There is a tangible mantle that accompanies faithful church service," they say, "and that mantle has been a boon to our home and our relationship."

When Elder Richard L. Evans quipped that he felt pangs of homesickness on the way to the airport outbound, he added that the coming home almost made the departure worth it. But what if the departures are so draining, so exhausting, so demanding that one only brings home the hulk, hardly an auspicious, alert, socially akin mate? Then there must be rejuvenation, pacing, and a place for the balance-staff.

9

The Self

Now let us look within the gospel for insight into the nature of man. Are we good? Are we bad? Are we neutral? Are we bundles of possibilities?

It is common to suppose that we have only two sets of inclinations or motivations: one good, one evil. On the good side are impulses to love, to help, to cooperate, to forbear, to be temperate, virtuous, kindly, humble, charitable. But we have another set. These are unwieldy, even ferocious impulses with such names as anger, lust, hate, vice, and all the counter-words in the religious vocabulary.

The United Self

But it is only in distortion that impulses divide us into warfare. Our nature is at root one, "and God having redeemed man from the fall, men became again, in their infant state, innocent before God" (D&C 93:38). Modern prophets teach that our entire throbbing collection of impulses, appetites, and passions may have a legitimate, goodly, even godly expression. Writes Parley P. Pratt:

> Man, know thy self,—study thine own nature,—learn thy powers of body,—thy capacity of mind. Learn thine origin, thy purpose and thy destiny. Study the true source of thine every happiness, and the happiness of all beings with which thou art associated. Learn to act in unison with thy true character, nature and attributes; and thus improve and cultivate the resources within and around thee. This will render you truly happy, and be an acceptable service to your God. And being faithful over a few things, you may hope to be made ruler over many things.
>
> Some persons have supposed that our natural affections were the results of a fallen and corrupt nature, and that they are "carnal, sensual, and devilish," and therefore ought to be resisted, subdued, or overcome as so many evils which prevent our perfection, or progress in the spiritual life. In short, that they should be greatly subdued in this world, and in the world to come entirely done away. And even our intelligence also.
>
> So far from this being the case, our natural affections are planted in us by the Spirit of God, for a wise purpose; and they are the very main-springs of life and happiness—they are the cement of all virtuous and heavenly society—they are the essence of charity, or love; and therefore never fail, but endure forever.
>
> There is not a more pure and holy principle in existence than the affection which glows in the bosom of a virtuous man for his companion; for his parents, brothers, sisters and children.
>
> If there be one scene in heaven or on earth, capable of calling forth the most refined sensibilities of our nature, it is the expressions of love which kindle into rapture, and which flow out in the soul of a woman towards her infant.
>
> What then is sinful? I answer, our unnatural passions and affections, or in other words the abuse, the perversion, the unlawful indulgence of that which is otherwise good. Sodom was not destroyed for their natural affections, but for the want of it. They had perverted all their affections, and had given place to that which was unnatural, and contrary to nature. Thus they had lost those holy and pure principles of virtue and love which were calculated to preserve and exalt.

Know then, O man, that aided and directed by the light of heaven the sources of thy happiness are within and around thee. Instead of seeking unto God for a mysterious change to be wrought, or for your affections and attributes to be taken away and subdued, seek unto him for aid and wisdom to govern, direct and cultivate them in a manner which will tend to your happiness and exaltation, both in this world and in that which is to come. Yea, pray to him that every affection, attribute, power and energy of your body and mind may be cultivated, increased, enlarged, perfected and exercised for his glory and for the glory and happiness of yourself, and of all those whose good fortune it may be to be associated with you. ("Intelligence and Affection," *Writings of Parley P. Pratt*, Salt Lake City, Parker Robinson, compiler.)

As Brigham Young had it, "Evil is inverted good." Lust, then, is simply love twisted and ripped away from its proper context. Our task, therefore, is not to beat one set of impulses into submission and feed another set until it flourishes. Our task is to transform all of our rooted impulses into the likeness of God. The actions and results and fruits that then emerge are not distorted gratifications but genuine fulfillments.

But do we have control of our feelings?

How free is free? Our cultures, our ordinary language, are loaded with assumptions that our thoughts, our feelings, are caused; and that those causes are outside ourselves. The choice here is not between man or mouse. It is between man and billiard ball. "You make me so mad." "You made me do it." "You are my problem. When you change, I'll change." (And not before!) But the gospel teaches that we are co-causes in a universe of cause and effect. The first step in solving any problem in marriage is to accept that the problem is yours, that you can change before your partner. The vital difference between reacting as a billiard ball does and responding as a child of God is freedom. We may "involuntarily" blink at an approaching fist. But as any young lady learns, blinking is not winking. Winking is purposive, meaningful, voluntary. Modern revelation makes it clear that we have power to direct or even reject, to honor or dishonor, to restrain or not restrain our impulses, even some "involuntary" ones.

"Behold, here is the agency of man, and here is the condemnation of man; because that which was from the beginning is plainly manifest unto them, and they receive not the light" (D&C 93:31).

The question, therefore, "Why do you do it?" has, in the end, a proper answer: "Because I choose!" If someone asks, "But *why* do you choose?" the answer to that in the end is also, "Because I choose." (Unless what is wanted is a list of things you thought about in deliberation *before* the decision. But they are not causes; they are reasons.) The very question, "But why?" makes a false assumption: that there is always something behind your choice which was the real "cause or causes" and that, therefore, you are always an effect, never a cause.

Equipped with this rationale it is easy to slip into the chain of blame. "Which do you think it is, Dad, heredity or environment?" the child says who brings home a terrible report card. Both the student and the father know there is another factor. None of us can escape being *influenced* by our backgrounds, as by our chromosomes. But our response to these at any point in our lives can modify the outcomes that might have occurred had we been automatons. More than that, we can modify our responses to our own responses. That is freedom. And it is eternal. And it means that in many cases we are deceiving ourselves when we say, "I can't help what I do."

What Is Selfishness?

Now let us come back to earth.

The prophets of our time have said that the fundamental problem in marriage, Latter-day Saint marriage, is selfishness, the attempt to get all we can get of happiness in defiance of the law that we are to lose ourselves.

In the cultures of the world, there is much that tells us otherwise: You are not to lose yourself in love for "the Lord" or your mate or your progeny. That is slavery. Instead do your thing, blow your mind, toot your horn, clamor for your rights, show contempt for everyone and everything that gets in the way. If your marriage is hard, you are certainly entitled to better. Therefore, break out, move on, and ignore the wreckage you leave behind. Intimidate, manipulate, protest, rebel, run away, hide.

We have the word of men and women who have been over this road (and sometimes the equally convincing evidence of anguished faces) that these are the ways of bitterness. They lead to diminished light, darkened gratifications, depressed consciousness and—dare we use the word?—yes, damnation. Damnation, as our revelations make clear, is the diminution of life—of abundant, full, rejoicing, fulfilling life which the Lord offers and wants for all of us.

We need comprehension of selfishness. In Nauvoo, the Prophet Joseph Smith was asked about self-aggrandizement. He said:

> Some people entirely denounce the principle of self-aggrandizement as wrong. But it is a correct principle, and may be indulged upon only one rule or plan—and that is to elevate, benefit and bless others first. If you will elevate others, the very work itself will exalt you. Upon no other plan can a man justly and permanently aggrandize himself.'' (*Young Woman's Journal*, vol. 2, p. 366.)

In a related sermon the Prophet once said, "Everything God does is to aggrandize his kingdom."

We have here a modern restatement of the teaching of the Master, "Whosoever shall lose his life for my sake and the gospel's, the same shall save it." This means there is a kind of selflessness which is self-fulfilling.

Divine Selfishness

So we must learn to give, to be outgoing, to give ourselves. But that profound truth has a matching one—we must learn to receive, to glory in blessedness (even when that blessedness is a mixture of the bitter and the sweet), and to sing at the burden of being both receptacle and transmitter. The gospel is good news: We may carry heavenly treasures even while we are flawed and foundering mortals.

Hugh Nibley has taught us a hymn of praise which may reflect the deep soul desires of Christ himself. These lines expand on a phrase in the apocryphal Gospel of Philip: "For he who has not the power to receive, how much more will he be unable to give?" It is a glimpse of what may have been a ritual pattern of the Last Supper. Jesus gathers his disciples and says:

> I wish to be saved and I wish to save.
> I wish to be delivered, and I wish to deliver.
> I wish to bear wounds and I wish to inflict them.
> I wish to be born and I wish to bring forth.
> I wish to eat and I wish to be eaten.
> I want to hear and I want to be heard.
> I want to comprehend, being all intelligence.
> I want to be washed, and I want to wash.
> I wish to pipe—dance all of you!
> I wish to mourn, all of you mourn.
> (Hugh Nibley, "The Early Christian Prayer
> Circle," *BYU Studies*, vol. 19, Fall 1978,
> pp. 41-78.)

Locked in these lines, whether they are historically authentic or not, is every dimension of marital and family love.

10

The Real Family

Only in recent times has the notion of the family become "nuclear," or at most two generations. Before that the word *family* meant all the presently visible family, usually four generations, plus the rootage family that reaches exponentially into the remote past. The decline of that wider vision is another symptom of the need for an Elijah to reverse that tide and to turn the hearts of the children to the fathers, all of the fathers and all of the mothers, until we break the bands of our confining here and now.

In both Jewish and Christian lore there are dozens of traditions and expectations of Elijah. He is somehow to restore the tribes of Jacob; he is to remove all impediments to peace; he is to restore the primal light which shone in Creation; he is to be the herald of the resurrection, to bring the Scheckinah into visibility, and to trumpet the complete perfection of the temple as Ezekiel described it; he is to adjust the law and biblical interpretation, to correct all genealogical records, to restore the vial of anointing oil which will have something to do with the Messiah. Such great miracles! Now one Jewish view of the great prophecy of Malachi (4:5-6):

> On that day [judgment day] all the children of the wicked who died in infancy on account of the sins of their fathers will be found among the just. But their fathers will be raised on the other side. The babes will implore their fathers to come to them. But God will not permit it. Then Elijah will go to the little ones and teach them how to plead in behalf of their fathers. They will stand before God: "Is not the measure of good, the mercy of God, larger than a measure of chastisements? If, then, we died for the sins of our fathers, should they not now for our sakes be granted the good and be permitted to join us in Paradise? God will give assent to their pleadings. And thus Elijah will have fulfilled the word of the Prophet Malachi. He will have brought back the fathers to the children. (Louis Ginsberg, *Legends of the Jews*, Philadelphia, Jewish Publication Society of America, 1954, p. 235.)

Thank God for a modern prophet who came to know the prophet Elijah and to receive through him powers whereby this moving result will extend—in a way few have thus far envisioned. But the word *turn* (Malachi 4:6) is also given as *seal*, and the word *seal* is also rendered as *reveal*. The spirit of Elijah will reveal, and turn, and seal the hearts of the fathers and the children to each other.

Says Joseph Smith:

> The spirit of Elijah is that degree of power which holds the sealing power of the kingdom to seal the hearts of the fathers to the children, and of the children to their fathers, not only on earth but in Heaven, both the living and the dead to each other, for they (the dead) cannot be made perfect without us. (Hebrews 11:40.) This power of Elijah is to that of Elias what, in the architecture of the temple of God, those who seal or cement the stone to their places are to those who cut or hew the stones, the one preparing the way for the other to accomplish the work. By this we are sealed with the Holy Spirit of promise that is, Elijah's. To obtain this sealing is to make our calling and

election sure, which we ought to give all diligence to accomplish. (From *Words of the Prophets*, 1841, Church Archives.)

It is not as individuals in solitary splendor that we come to such levels of sealing. The sealing relates to all who have preceded us and all those who follow us. Who wants to take on such a mountain of responsibility? The Saints of the latter days. And if, by the quality of our lives (and not just by vicarious ordinance work), we break our clouded inheritance by righteousness, we may reach generation after generation of those who have, as President Spencer W. Kimball says, "walked in muddy places" and lived and died with neither a lot of light or a lot of love. Then, and only then, can we be sure of our own place in the chain.

Brigham Young said: "If our hearts are turned to our fathers— don't you see, their hearts will be turned to us. It is necessary to have a regular chain clear back to Adam, and we have commenced it, and if we are faithful we shall accomplish it." (Discourse of Sunday, March 12, 1848.) (See Joseph Smith's comments on revealing the covenants of the fathers in relation to the children and the covenants of the children in relation to the fathers—*Teachings*, p. 321.)

We are taught that the song we will sing together, the new song, at the second coming of Christ will include these sentences:

The Lord hath brought again Zion;
The Lord hath redeemed his people, Israel,
According to the election of grace,
Which was brought to pass *by the faith*
And covenant of their fathers. (See D&C 84:99.)

They have done for us what we could not do for ourselves. We are to do for them what they cannot do for themselves.

In the first wedding ceremony given by revelation to the Prophet Joseph Smith—prior to the completion of the temple— the "giving" of daughter or son in marriage is done in the name of the parents but also of all the "holy progenitors" and then sealed in the name of the Lord, whereby all these powers are to

"concentrate in you and through you to your posterity forever."
(Nauvoo, Illinois, July 27, 1842.)

The Veiled Family

It is a paradox of our time that we are bombarded day and night by mass communication yet suffer severe loneliness. Some universities now have "computer counseling"—you insert a punched card and read the printout. Loneliness is intensified by a feeling of having once been in touch, in communion, that harmony having since been broken. Of this there is a spiritual equivalent. One of our writers calls it "celestial homesickness."

Is there any release or relief? Yes; the recognition that the separation is not absolute. This theme occupied Joseph Smith in the late years of his prophetic ministry. He taught that communion with the spirit world was one of the high privileges of the Restoration. The conventional negative faith that "when you are dead you are dead" is replaced among Latter-day Saints with the faith that our loved ones are not only somewhere but here. Speaking of the spirits of the just, Joseph Smith testified: "Enveloped in flaming fire, they are not far from us, and know and understand our thoughts, feelings, and motions, and are often pained [and rejoiced] therewith." (See *Teachings*, p. 326.)

Whether from our vantage point the veil between us is thick or thin, we are surrounded in profound ways.

Note these key sentences:

The heavenly priesthood . . . are not idle spectators (*Teachings*, p. 232).

We must have revelation from them (*Teachings*, p. 338).

We may look for angels and receive their ministrations (*Teachings*, p. 161).

We may come to the general assembly and church of the first born—Spirits of Just men made perfect, unto Christ. . . . It is our privilege to pray for and obtain these things. (*The Words of Joseph Smith*, p. 14.)

I assure the Saints that truth, in reference to these matters, can and may be known through the revelations of God in the way of His ordinances, and in answer to prayer (*Teachings*, p. 325).

We underestimate, I believe, the enduring influence of "those beyond." Through it separations and estrangements and losses and tragedies are tempered. For example, Wilford Woodruff lost a son in a drowning accident. The Spirit manifested to him and his wife, Phoebe, that "now we have an angel in the spirit world." And he was privileged (it was one of his spiritual gifts) to know something of the son's continuing activities. (See *Wilford Woodruff,* p. 499, and Abraham H. Cannon journal, January 2, 1894— BYU Special Collections.) He later taught: "The Lord gives his angels charge concerning us . . . and they do all in their power for our salvation" (*Young Woman's Journal* 5:551).

Parley P. Pratt wrote of the pure in heart that when the "outward organs of thought and perception" are at rest (when we are asleep or almost asleep) the spirit world draws close and we receive messages of comfort and reproof as well as solicitude of affection. "Spirit communes with spirit, thought meets thought, soul blends with soul in all the raptures of mutual, pure, and eternal love" (*Key to the Science of Theology,* London, 1855, pp. 119-21). One such experience enabled him to endure a dismal dungeon in Missouri.

Elder John A. Widtsoe records impressive experiences of his temple life in sealing sessions (he had been promised as a boy that he would have "great faith in the ordinances of the Lord's house"). Bereaved in the untimely deaths of several of his children, he had covenanted with the Lord to give this "family time" to "the youth of the Church." His writings glow with the conviction that no other Church requirement does so much to bridge the gap of separation, to renew one's feeling of worth and belonging, to regain spiritual power that fits one for the deprivations and travails of this life.

Elder Orson F. Whitney, eighteen years after his wife Zina's death, felt one evening a "soft and gentle touch," then saw her. "She was hovering over me . . . It was all so real. I could not doubt that she was actually there." (Orson F. Whitney, *Through Memory's Halls,* Independence, Missouri, Zion's Printing, 1930, p. 413.)

Bishop Marriner W. Merrill prayed almost in despair when a son, whose father was dead, ran away from home. In a dream he saw the boy's exposure to the worst vices of the world. But he saw that "a light followed him." The light, he was told, was the influence of the boy's father, which "would preserve him from doing any evil which could cut him off from a chance to return to the fold of Christ." (*Young Woman's Journal*, 11:56.) Eventually the boy returned and more. He helped others to return.

When Jedediah M. Grant was given his glimpse of the "next sphere," he saw that it was a place of superlative order and harmony. The core of that order was family "organized in family capacities." He also beheld that members of some families were not permitted to dwell together "because they had not honored their callings here." So keen was the impress of this revelation upon his spirit that he asked to return to his body in order to report and reinforce this mighty recognition to his children. They listened but hardly heard. They thought he was hallucinating in his final hours. "Perhaps it is so. And perhaps not," they said. (*Journal of Discourses*, 4:135; Brigham Young's Manuscript History, December 4, 1856.) But the truth had reached Jedediah's soul indelibly as it should reach ours: Spirits do not cease caring when they pass through the veil. Nor do covenant bonds disintegrate.

Lonely and estranged parents, or those who are denied the full scope of family life (and the more we look at it carefully the more we realize that all of us, for all of our blessings, are in a condition of denial) can be heartened by the testimony of modern prophets: The processes of surrogate parenting—reaching out to others—can have the same eventual blessedness as firsthand flesh-and-blood parenting. The Prophet Joseph Smith once comforted the hearts of Abraham O. Smoot and his wife, who had adopted a little boy, that their constant vigil of love and nurture would eventually result in that child's being "as if" their own flesh and blood.

And those are two of the most powerful words in the gospel vocabulary: "as if." One who lived without the full blessings of the gospel can now vicariously receive the ordinances "as if" he had. One who is denied one or another or both of his parents can live on "as if" both were present in his life. One who has no immediate access to the temple can live "as if" he did. And there is heavenly sanction for all of these privileges.

Eliza R. Snow, devastated in the sudden, stark death of the Prophet Joseph Smith, was brought down to a grief that came out in one prayer—"Let me die also." After such severing, why go on? Her prayer was answered: "No." Instead by a communing glimpse of Joseph she was reassured of eventual reunion. And she was recommitted to fill her calling (she had no children of her own) by reaching out to the needy around her. The life-giving effect of that glimpse took her through not a day or a week but rather through three decades.

It is common in our psychological age to suppose these accounts are but a wishful refusal to face reality. But reality is what is real. And relationships are real. And these experiences are the result of the kinds of relationship all of us are commanded to live for.

11

The Little Things

T he little foxes destroy the vines." And it is the Spirit that giveth life.

One of our leaders has said, "In marriage the big things are the little things and the little things are the big things." A hug, for instance, is a small thing. But there are studies showing that every child needs about one hug an hour, at least twelve a day, to be reassured and secure in love. Another study shows that even for us "grown-ups," every negative put-down requires fourteen resounding put-ups to counterbalance. Otherwise we tend to esteem the putter-downer as our enemy.

We who are assigned to teach and lead and correct should understand this, the Lord's revealed law: "Show forth an increase of love" (D&C 121:43). "Love begets love. Let us pour forth love." (*Teachings*, p. 316.) If love surrounds a rebuke, the rebuke will be accepted. If an apparent *decrease* of love glares through our counsels or corrections, we may plead until our faces are blue— to no effect except stiffening, hardening, alienation.

To couples in the temple marriage, President David O. McKay often gave counsel which had grown out of his own long and perceptive home life. To some, what he said seemed trivial, seemed to be of little things. Experience had made him wiser than they.

He spoke of three virtues as "contributive to the perpetuity of love," which otherwise becomes fragile. He cited the psalm of love (1 Corinthians 13 in the New Testament) which celebrates all three:

First, "Love suffereth long, is kind."

You have been happy, he would say, to anticipate each other's wishes before marriage. Continue to do so in kindness. Eternal marriage is eternal courtship. Both husband and wife will appreciate kindness, gentleness. Kindness is not the highest virtue. Love is. God is love. And perhaps the second greatest virtue is compassion. But kindness is a diamond among the jewels, abiding and priceless.

Second, courtesy. "Love seeketh not her own."

This is, the President said, kindness in action. But it counts. The little considerations, neglected, can break up a marriage. He spoke of a man who had turned against his wife because "in public she made me feel she was ashamed of me." Attend to the social graces. Open the door for your wife. Help with her coat, the chair, the door. Be patient when your wife is buying a dress. Never tell a story that will cause a pang in your companion. Courtesy is most neglected in the place where it should reign— the home.

Third, trust. "Love believeth all things."

"Your bride," the President would say, "is clean. I speak it of her reverently. Both of you begin this day a sacred trust. You may be on opposite sides of the world, but let your hearts beat in unison. In the most sacred of buildings you have made a covenant with each other. Keep yourselves for each other. This is the highest ideal of marriage ever given to man. You will learn to appreciate it more and more. The flower of love is grounded in trust. Even a passing suspicion can wilt it."

In the book *Home Memories of President David O. McKay*, the President summed up: "Love, as the body, must have nourishment or it will starve. There is no great thing the man or woman can do to keep *love* alive and healthy, but there are many little things given daily and, if possible, hourly—a kind word, a courteous act, a smile, an endearing term, a sparkle in the eye, an unexpected service, a birthday greeting, a remembering of the wedding anniversary—these and a hundred other seemingly insignificant deeds and expressions are the food upon which love thrives." (Quoted in Rex Skidmore, *I Thee Wed*, Deseret Book, 1964, p. 11.)

The President embodied his own counsel.

"I don't think," a rather cynical man said to President McKay, "that there is one truly happy married couple in the world."

"I know of one," the President retorted.

"Who?"

"Rae and I."

"Oh," said the man, "but you're always away traveling for the Church."

President McKay recounted this incident and the ways his family dealt with frequent separations. (His call to the Twelve came when he was only thirty-two.) There were ways of keeping touch and there were joyous homecomings. In addition, the couple held inviolate over many decades this one pattern: Each Friday night was theirs together, a time for both of them to anticipate and count on; a time to freshen up and revive courtings; a time for a pleasant restaurant or the theater. That one certainty in their consciousness helped them past the "everlasting something else" that drains the energies of parents and leaves them neither time nor talent for each other.

Elevating the Funny Bone

A striking legend describes Adam and Eve just as they were about to depart from the Garden, venturing as the vanguard couple into the world below. There were solemn embraces and good-byes. Just before the couple disappeared in the distant mists, the Father, knowing better than they what was ahead for them, could not stand it. He called them back—and gave them a sense of humor.

Few of us think of humor as a spiritual gift. This, no doubt, because humor attends comedy, which we think of as frivolous (even when, as it often is, it is more profound than tragedy); and because our own modern scriptures counsel us against light-mindedness and in favor of being sober and vigilant. But humor may be spiritual. It is unifying. It is part of healthy love. Its absence leads to unhealthy brittleness.

We are counseled against light-mindedness, the betrayal or abuse or mocking of the sacred. But we are counseled *toward* lightheartedness, toward "cheerful hearts and countenances" (D&C 59:15). Humor can lighten our load and our face at every age and stage. The family that often laughs together, lasts together.

A special value attaches to the capacity to laugh at ourselves and at what is foolish, ridiculous, or awkward in situations.

It brings freshness, zest, imagination and creativity to marriage. It can move mountains by shrinking them down to their actual size—molehills. And it can help us avoid all kinds of unnecessary collision. Children love to be released by humor from the ceaseless bombardment of serious and super-serious discipline. So do grown-up children.

It is said that a sober young man once approached President Harold B. Lee and told him he had a message for the entire Church. President Lee responded, "Young man, I'm not going to question your experience. But I have noticed something since you came into my office. You haven't smiled once. And anyone who takes himself that seriously is not very receptive to the Lord." The story, apocryphal or not, underlines a truth: there is an intimate connection between spirituality and humor. Together they can be defined as susceptibility not only to divine influences but to the human and humane around us. Especially to that within our own skins.

Our history is replete with examples of men and women—Joseph Smith preeminently—who could move from being "playful and cheerful" in the midst of affliction to being inspired and attuned to heaven amidst the "solemnities of eternity." President Hugh B. Brown is one example. Faltering on his ninety-year-old legs, he was approached by a sympathetic Elder Boyd K. Packer. "May I be your cane? the latter said, extending his arm. "Yes," said President Brown, "if I am Abel."

Coming infirm and weak down the aisle of a chapel, he was approached by a little old lady who burst out, "Oh, President Brown, I have always wanted you to speak at my funeral." "Sister," he replied, "If you want me to speak at your funeral, you'd better hurry."

Then there was that most serious moment when, after he had a stroke, his family surrounded his bed, expecting, as the doctor predicted, that he would not survive the night. Early in the morning he rallied. One eye half opened and slowly surveyed the anxious faces. A slight twist showed in the corner of his lips as he said, "I fooled you."

If you can laugh at yourself, you will make it much easier on your companion and on your children, who have to live with what you do and don't do and with what you are and are not.

12

Solving,
Resolving,
and Dissolving

One can speak of "solving" the problems of marriage. But where the problems derive from long-standing habits of attitude and of feeling, there is no "quick fix." They respond only to long-range and increasing healthy-mindedness and spiritual deepening.

Again and again we participate in programs designed to change *behavior*. Within limits they have wholesome and lasting effects. But the announced intent of Christ in the transformation of man and family is far more inclusive. It is to change behavers, to change our souls in nature, in inclination, in desire. That is like replacing the tissues and bones of a person while he is still alive. It is like rebuilding a ship at sea. But again and again we see the process at work, personalities illumined and purified through the renovating powers of the gospel. We see "hopeless problems" diminish. We see them fade away as a nightmare does.

A marriage which is attemptedly built on a foundation other than gospel principles not only probably will not last; in the larger sense, it will not live. It attempts the impossible: to derive life from non-life. Persons sometimes say, "When I get my job and my home life straightened out, then I can take a look at religion." Instead it works the other way: When you get your religious life attuned, home and job will be renewed and revitalized.

Where Does One Go for Help?

Rarely has there been a culture or a time when there was so much specialized analysis and poll taking and open-ended interviewing and therapeutic devices. And have there ever been as many clinics and workshops and seminars and practitioners of "Can this marriage be saved?" In some places divorce is not sanctioned until couples at least make some effort toward solving or dissolving their problems through professional channels.

It is not our purpose to discount any of these services. When couples are in need they are in need. And the first step is to acknowledge the need.

What we wish to reassert and remind our readers of (for it is already known in our heart of hearts) is that the two greatest problem-solvers in any individual life are the person himself and the God who gave him life.

What are the main impediments to all this? Where are the hang-ups?

As Stephen Covey and I have traveled and listened, and even encouraged persons to submit anonymously three-by-five cards designating their toughest problem or most recurring frustration, a pattern developed. Let us here briefly respond to some of the most recurrent difficulties and the gospel way out.

Dealing with Conflict

We all come to the marriage state as incomplete persons. We come with wounds, with over- and under-sensitivities, with tendencies brought from former generations, and with both realistic and impossible expectations. Conclusion: There will always be need for adjustments. To a degree, husband and wife should see both their roles as physician to patient, as someone equipped to nurture and heal.

Candidly, in our traveling and observing Stephen Covey and I have encountered no marriage in which the partners are happy only "because of." If they are happy, it is also "in spite of." The rumor of families who have "never spoken a cross word" to each other persists; but we have yet to meet one. Couples who are making it have conflict. The difference is that they have ways of living with it. "We have not avoided spats and arguments. We have not even avoided arguing in front of the children. What we observe is that sometimes a thundershower clears the air. It helps us get our feelings out in the open. Then we try to compose things."

Couples report three ways to nip destructive, hurtful argument in the bud:

1. The first, a thought by President Spencer W. Kimball, is represented in the accompanying diagram. It indicates that marriage is like two overlapping ellipses. The center part of the diagram is the area where each is in harmony with the other, with fully shared mutuality. But at each end is an area where there is no overlapping, a kind of no-man's land and no-woman's land. By all means these areas should be worked on to reduce their size, but to the extent that they are not brought into the overlap portion, partners had best learn simply to avoid those explosive areas.

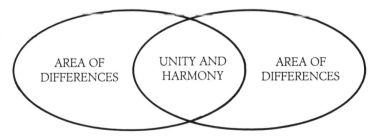

AREA OF DIFFERENCES   UNITY AND HARMONY   AREA OF DIFFERENCES

2. The second way is getting to the knees in prayer and each "praying out" his feelings with the partner listening. "When I am angry, the first thing I do is pray," said one of our great patriarchs. "And I am never so angry but what I can pray."

3. Simply pulling away, one or the other, not in a "pouting" stance but in a quiet resolve (which both have approved in the past) to postpone discussing the vexing issue until there is more composure.

Again and again we have seen that the expectation of total overlap is faulty, and the present failures to achieve are a carrying of an unnecessary burden. There cannot be mutuality, or what Stephen Covey calls interdependence, unless there is also a measure of autonomy and distinction. Individuality can enrich marriage. But not if it is a constant rasp, with one mate trying to push the other into an impossible mold.

Forgiveness

Everywhere we have candid interviews *after* our seminars, we find unforgiveness.

The song says it—we always hurt the one (or ones) we love. Yet we have a commandment as ringing and unqualified as a bell: We are required to forgive and seek forgiveness—perpetually—for the hurt. Especially husbands. Especially wives. Especially children.

"Bear it patiently," says the Lord, if not, "it shall be accounted unto you as being meted out as a just measure unto you." (D&C 98:24.)

In recent years scientific confirmation has vindicated this teaching of Christ: Love cannot flourish without forgiveness. This is so not because unforgiveness is bitter and painful for the other person (though it often is). It is because unforgiveness is self-destructive in the person who harbors it.

This is one of the eternal laws. We know it from the experiences of the Brethren who are in touch with those who are divorced, the yet unmarried, and the widowed, as well as the "barely-holding marrieds." Many cling to resentments toward both their former or would-be mates and their children. Even toward God himself. These long-lasting resentments become a cumulative catalog of grievances their hearts constantly dwell and feed upon.

One of the most forgiving of men, Reed Bradford, says, "Forgiveness is not hard at all once you really have the Spirit of Christ." But there is the rub.

The Lord gave us a revelation on *how* we can forgive. It is in his admonition, "pray *for* your enemies." Notice he does not say *pray against* your enemies. In rare circumstances we may catalog the grievances and put the name of the perpetrator at the top of our prayer list and then ask the Lord to come down in justice. In extremities, where life is at stake, the Lord has permitted this procedure. But not against those with whom we have been called to be one flesh. Not ever. Instead we are to forgive seventy times seven. That seems a great burden to those of us who have not even done it once.

In short, when someone treats you like dirt, you treat them like gold. After praying for, the Master admonishes us, we are to "do good to" those who despitefully use us. You are asked, when you feel put upon or offended or ignored or treated like a "thing" instead of a person, to heap good on the offender. In both the short and the long run that is your best hope. It will prevent poisons from entering you and ill feeling will disappear. Such prayer, such action, requires two kinds of trust in the Lord: trust that returning good for evil is best for everyone; trust that the promise that you will have peace of soul will one day extend to the person you are willing to so serve. And it will return to you.

In a celebrated but misnamed film the closing line is "Love means not having to say you are sorry." The truth is, we are learning, the other way around. We inflict hurts by neglect, by pique, or by spite. Of course, the words are not the point. The intent in the heart is—the forgiving attitude before, during, and after grievances, even when they come in battalions. "Pray for your (seeming) enemy." And in your very prayer you will begin to feel the spirit of Stephen, who cried out "Lay not this sin to their charge" even as the jagged rocks struck and cut open his flesh.

Were Christ himself in the room when you bear ill feelings, would his influence subdue you? Would your love for him enable you to see as he sees the victim of your spite? And if so, would you cry out "Forgive me my unforgiveness!" Or would you still insist on blighting your own soul as you mutter, "I will never forgive you for that as long as I live!"

The Father of us all—so the Prophet Joseph knew by vision as by experience—forbears, persists in mercy, because as the revelation says, "thou art gracious and merciful, and wilt turn away thy wrath when thou lookest upon the face of thine Anointed" (D&C 109:53). Has there ever been a time in your home when as you were about to administer punishment one of your family cried out, "Please, no!" Were you dissuaded? Vicarious suffering is real. Children may offer to make it up, to fill in, even (if it were possible) to atone. The smallest of children demonstrate such impulses. Are we not commanded to become as a little child?

But what if the person I am expected to forgive does not show the least signs of repentance or change? What if I forgive and am not forgiven? What if it is about time justice took over?

It would be much easier if the commandment were "Forgive only when there is proof of repentance." But the revelation says we are "required to forgive all men." *All* is an inclusive word.

President John Taylor once found a way to teach a judgmental young member of the Twelve that forgiveness is in advance of justice and that the Spirit of the Lord manifests the Lord's yearning for all of us to eliminate the spirit of hatred and bitterness. In a headlined story a prominent Church leader had been excommunicated and now had asked for rebaptism. President Taylor wrote a letter to the Twelve asking for their recommendation. One man held out against rebaptism. President Taylor asked him why, and he said, "While I live I never expect to consent if it is left to my judgment. . . . I can tell the Lord that he had disgraced this Church enough, and that I did not propose to let any such man come back into the Church."

The apostle then went home for lunch. He picked up his *Doctrine and Covenants* and it opened to, "Wherefore, I say unto you, that ye ought to forgive one another; for he that forgiveth not his brother his trespasses standeth condemned before the Lord. . . . I, the Lord, will forgive whom I will forgive, but of you it is required to forgive all men." (D&C 64:9-10.)

The apostle returned to President Taylor and told him he had changed his mind. Elated, President Taylor said, "How did you feel when you left here an hour ago? Did you feel that you wanted to hit that man right squarely between the eyes and knock him down?"

"That is just the way I felt."

"How do you feel now?"

"Well, to tell you the truth, President Taylor, I hope the Lord will forgive the sinner."

The President said, "You feel very happy, don't you, in comparison? You had the spirit of anger, you had the spirit of bitterness in your heart toward that man, because of his sin and because of the disgrace he had brought upon the Church. And now you have the spirit of forgiveness and you really feel happy, don't you?"

That apostle was Heber J. Grant. And he learned his lesson. (See *Gospel Standards,* compiled by G. Homer Durham, Deseret News Press, 1943, pp. 260-62.)

At the first organization of the Relief Society, Joseph pleaded for kindness, charity and love. He told the sisters to let their administrations "be confined mostly to those around you." Their knowledge might expand to the whole world, but the need was in those closest to them. Then he said, "It grieves me that there is no fuller fellowship, if one member suffers all [should] feel it, by union of feeling we obtain power with God. . . . Nothing is so much calculated to lead people to forsake sin, as to take them by the hand and watch over them with tenderness.'' (Meeting of June 9, 1842, minutes of the organization of Relief Society, Church Archives, p. 226.)

Often the question is asked, How do I know when I have forgiven? The experienced among us can say with Elder Heber J. Grant in answer: When *you* feel at peace. When *you* feel compassion instead of vindictiveness (the closer we come to the Lord, the greater our compassion for perishing souls). When anger is gone.

Elder George F. Richards shared this example of forgiveness in extremity.

> I dreamed that I and a group of my own associates found ourselves in a courtyard where, around the outer edge of it, were German soldiers —and Führer Adolph Hitler was there with his group, and they seemed to be sharpening their swords and cleaning their guns, and making preparations for a slaughter of some kind, or an execution. We knew not what, but, evidently we were the objects. But presently a circle was formed and this Führer and his men were all within the circle, and my group and I were circled on the outside, and he was sitting on the inside of the circle with his back to the outside, and when we walked around and I got directly opposite to him, I stepped inside the circle and walked across to where he was sitting, and spoke to him in a manner something like this:
>
> "I am your brother. You are my brother. In our heavenly home we lived together in love and peace. Why can we not so live here on the earth?"
>
> And it seemed to me that I felt in myself, welling up in my soul, a love for that man, and I could feel that he was having the same experience, and presently he arose, and we embraced each other and kissed each other, a kiss of affection.
>
> Then the scene changed so that our group was within the circle, and he and his group were on the outside, and when he came around to where I was standing, he stepped inside the circle and embraced me again, with a kiss of affection.

I think the Lord gave me that dream. Why should I dream of this man, one of the greatest enemies of mankind, and one of the wickedest, but that the Lord should teach me that I must love my enemies, and I must love the wicked as well as the good?

Now, who is there in this wide world that I could not love under those conditions, if I could only continue to feel as I felt then? I have tried to maintain this feeling and, thank the Lord, I have no enmity toward any person in this world; I can forgive all men, so far as I am concerned, and I am happy in doing so and in the love which I have for my fellow men.

I love the Saints of God, as I love the Lord and his work. I love you faithful men and women who are laboring for the Lord, and for your fellow men. (George F. Richards, *Conference Report*, April 1950, pp. 139-40.)

Before Final Rupture

Regrettably there are circumstances in which persistently intolerable behavior by an unrepentant partner makes divorce inevitable. Where this is not so, where the persuasions of reason and time and the Spirit can be used to change the heart and mind and behavior, the longest-term advantages stand out as the distant but persistent motivators to solutions of marital problems. In other words, the life hereafter overshadows this one.

Elder Erastus Snow recalls a saying of the Prophet Joseph: "The Holy Ghost or Spirit of the Lord underlies all of the natural senses, viz., seeing, hearing, smelling, tasting and touching. This Spirit communicates with the spirit of man, and enlivens all the other senses."

And what is the eventual outcome? Joseph Smith answers: "Would you think it strange if I relate what I have seen in vision in relation to this interesting theme? Those who have died in Jesus Christ may expect to enter into all that fruition of joy when they come forth, which they possessed or anticipated here. Let these truths sink down in our hearts, that we may even here begin to enjoy that which shall be in full hereafter. Hosanna . . . to

Almighty God, that rays of light begin to burst forth upon us even now." (*Teachings*, p. 295-96.)

Of the hereafter, Brigham Young, though often labeled as an utterly practical man, was also a visionary man. He knew whereof Joseph Smith spoke. When two sisters came to him at the end of their rope, unable to see any way out except divorce, he lifted their sights. His witness gives pause to those of us who tend to imbibe two harmful drugs: self-pity and hasty judgment. He said:

> I think it has been taught by some that as we lay our bodies down, they will so rise again in the resurrection with all the impediments and imperfections that they had here; and that if a wife does not love her husband in this state she cannot love him in the next. This is not so. Those who attain to the blessing of the first or celestial resurrection will be pure and holy, and perfect in body. Every man and woman that reaches to this unspeakable attainment will be as beautiful as the angels that surround the throne of God. (*Journal of Discourses*, vol. 10:24.)

And elsewhere he said:

> If that dissatisfied wife could behold the transcendent beauty of person, the Godlike qualities of the resurrected husband that she now despises, her love for him would be unbounded and unutterable. Instead of despising him, she would feel like worshipping him, he is so holy, so pure, so perfect, so filled with God in his resurrected body. There will be no dissatisfaction of this kind in the resurrection of the just. The faithful elders [will] have then proved themselves worthy of their wives and are prepared to be crowned gods, to be filled with all the attributes of the gods that dwell in the future eternity. Could the dissatisfied ones see a vision, even, of the future glorified state of their husbands, love for them would immediately spring up within you, and no circumstance could prevail upon you to forsake them. (*Discourse of Brigham Young*, October 8, 1861.)

This teaching does not contradict a related one that we carry into the spirit world "the same spirit," and presumably the same habits and predispositions, that were our characteristics here.

The spirit world is but an extension of our earthly probation. Full judgment is not rendered until resurrection. All the story is not written yet. In the meantime we are counseled by those who know whereof they speak, "Do not give up, do not give up loving, do not give up hoping."

In one of his most protracted sermons on the difficulties of marriage, President Spencer W. Kimball told a huge assembly of youth that when the wife is taken off the pedestal and put on a budget, when foibles in our partners thrust themselves upon us, romantic expectations are shaken to the core. But to this lengthy warning of the challenges of marriage he added an electrifying sentence: "Yet out of it can come the highest ecstasy of which men and women are capable." So it is.

At our seminars Stephen Covey and I are often asked whether the gospel is one of duty, discipline, and self-denial; or one of fulfillment, self-realization, and joy. We answer, yes. We are aware of no radiant marriages that do not demonstrate both. Christ's life demonstrates both. The world is full of people who hope to beat the system. The system is beating them.

How do we know we have the Spirit? Joseph Smith said:

> They can tell the Spirit of the Lord from all other spirits; it will whisper peace and joy to their souls; it will take malice, hatred, strife and all evil from their hearts; and their whole desire will be to do good, bring forth righteousness and build up the kingdom of God . . . Be sure and tell the people to keep the Spirit of the Lord. (Preston Nibley, *Exodus to Greatness*, Deseret Book, 1947, p. 379.)

Brigham Young often observed that he had tried to erase the word *sacrifice* from his vocabulary. (This is the man who served nine missions and had been mobbed out of five homes.) Will we really call it a sacrifice, he asked, if we "sacrifice death for life, darkness for light, error for truth, doubt and unbelief for knowledge and the certainty of the things of God! To give a penny for a billion of gold, to give a handful of earth for a planet, to exchange this temporary worn-out tenement for one glorified that will continue to abide and increase throughout a never-ending eternity!" ("Remarks at the St. George Temple," *Young Woman's Journal,* vol. 17, p. 253.)

"If you want to govern a world," Brigham Young said to an ambitious man, "learn to love your wife."

Elder Joseph Fielding Smith has written:

> I do not care what *office* you hold in this Church—you may be an apostle, you may be a patriarch, a high priest, or anything else—you cannot receive the *fulness of the priesthood* unless you go into the temple of the Lord and receive these ordinances of which the Prophet speaks. *No man can get the fulness of the priesthood outside of the temple of the Lord. . . .*
>
> To obtain the fulness of the priesthood does not mean that a man must become President of the Church. Every man who is faithful and will receive these ordinances and blessings obtains a fulness of the priesthood, and the Lord has said "he makes them equal in power, and in might, and in dominion." (D&C 76:95, 88:107.) Only one man at a time on the earth holds the *keys* of the priesthood; only one man at a time has the power to receive revelations for the Church; but the Lord has made it possible for every man in this Church, through his obedience, to receive the fulness of the priesthood through the ordinances of the temple of the Lord. This cannot be received anywhere else. (*Doctrines of Salvation,* Bookcraft, 1956, vol. 3, pp. 131-33.)

And this priesthood fulness can only be exercised in righteousness. The restored gospel of Jesus Christ not only tempers but replaces the rampant drive for power, domination, manipulation. It replaces it with the image of a compassionate servant whose powers diminish and weaken until he learns that his calling and destiny is not to "lord it over" but to "lord it under," to descend below all things in order to lift, heal, redeem. That is Christlike. And Christ is Godlike.

13

What It Means to Be Sealed

Our generation has become a set of psychological hypochondriacs. We know the labels and throw them around with athletic ease: It is easy to get the impression that we must live under frenetic tension, that security is unavailable, that no relationship can be sustained for very long, that experimentation is the name of the game, that there is nothing we can really count on, not even in love. And that "that's the way the cookie crumbles."

The truth? There is something to count on, something that may *abide* in our hearts. Amidst the unknowns and the inevitable mortal risks and suspense, the gospel of Jesus Christ promises us certitude, foundations upon which we can build with unwavering confidence and from which we cannot, regardless of the surging tides or storms, be ripped away. "Ye are built upon my rock" (3 Nephi 18:12), Jesus said to the Twelve in ancient America. The rock is a person. It is he. In modern times he has said to us: "Wherefore, I am in your midst, and I am the good shepherd, and the stone of Israel. He that buildeth upon this rock shall never fall." (D&C 50:44.) He is a flowing rock, a living rock, the Rock of Heaven (Moses 7:53). "And none of them that my Father hath given me shall be lost" (D&C 50:42).

The following exchange of letters occurred when Heber C. Kimball had been called upon his eighth mission (in June 1843). Before his departure his wife Vilate penned these words.

Nauvoo, June 8th, 1843

My Ever Kind and Affectionate Companion:

I write these few lines for you to look upon when you are far and distant from me, and when you read them remember they were penned by one whose warm, affectionate heart is ever the same toward you; yea, *it is fixed, firm as a decree which is unalterable.* Therefore, let your heart be comforted, and if you never more behold my face in time, let this be my last covenant and testimony unto you: that I am yours in time and throughout all eternity. This blessing has been sealed upon us by the Holy Spirit of promise, and cannot be broken only through transgression, or committing a grosser crime than your heart or mine is capable of, that is, murder.

So be of cheer, my dearest dear,
    For we shall meet again
Where all our sorrows will be o'er,
    And we are free from pain.

V. Kimball

Heber's full heart responded with a prayer-letter:

O God, the Eternal Father, in the name of Jesus Christ wilt Thou bless her with peace and with a long life; and when Thou shalt see fit to take her, let Thy servant go with her; and dwell with each other throughout all eternity; that no power shall ever separate us from each other; for Thou, O God, knowest we love each other with pure hearts. Still, we are willing to leave each other from time to time, to preach Thy word to the children of men. Now, O God, hear Thy servant, and let us have the desires of our hearts; for we want to live together, and die, and be buried, and rise and reign together in Thy

Kingdom with our dear children; in the name of Jesus Christ of Nazareth. Amen.

(Above letters from *The Life of Heber C. Kimball,* by Orson F. Whitney, Bookcraft, 1973, p. 335.)

To receive such a seal, to know that the binding power of love attended by this Spirit of God "is fixed, firm as a decree which is unalterable"—to know that this blessing is sealed in the very heavens—this is an anchor which Joseph Smith taught "would sustain the soul in every time of trial, trouble, and tribulation."

It is a proper footnote that one of the last prophecies that fell from Heber's lips came as he walked behind Vilate's coffin: "I shall not be long after her." And he was not.

14

Peace

Peace I leave with you."

Jesus said he would leave us peace but that he would not give it as the world gives peace. The world still seeks peace in barricades, bombs, and returning "measure for measure." But if our hearts are not to be troubled, and not to be afraid, then from out of our hearts must go the desire for vengeance. That is the most mighty change that can occur in the entire universe. It is so because it changes everything. And it stops the chain of retaliation. In marriage it stops what Stephen Covey calls "fight or flight."

Knowing the trauma that was about to engulf those who had struggled to be his disciples, Jesus said to them, as in modern times he has said to us, "I will not leave you comfortless." He left them, but he did not leave them. The Comforter came and brought peace.

In the ashes of our anger or other distress Jesus Christ will grant *us* peace.

Grant what?

Peace.

In some remote future?

No. The good news is "peace in *this* world." That means peace in *our* world, peace in the quiet turning of our own private interior selves. (See D&C 59.)

He who controlled the elements by a word can control the ragings of pique and spite and enmity in a man's heart by the Spirit that gives efficacy to the word.

> So when our lives are clouded o'er
> And storm winds drift us from the shore,
> Say, lest we sink to rise no more,
> "Peace, be still."

Stephen R. Covey

for practical

15

The Supreme
Importance of an
Eternal Perspective

I hope that by now, as the reader you feel uplifted and inspired with a sense of the exalted place marriage and family rightfully have in the eternal scheme of things. I hope also that the cumulative effect of the many quoted sayings and teachings of modern-day apostles and prophets has been powerfully persuasive in testifying of the gospel solution to marriage and family challenges and problems. That is the essence, the essential message, the bottom line, of this book. While we are both attempting to teach that essence in the form of correct principles, Truman Madsen's primary focus is on the concepts and the philosophy, and mine is on the application and the practice.

This chapter is to serve as a transition between the two parts of the book, expressing first the authors' conviction that by far the most practical, realistic, and helpful thing one can do is to inculcate within himself an eternal frame of reference. Such a spiritual mindset is absolutely imperative in either properly understanding or properly applying the different practical suggestions in the later chapters of this book. Otherwise the techniques will lose both their efficacy or power and their harmony with each other. Without an eternal perspective we will simply not be able to endure or sustain the inevitable rigors, struggles, and challenges of married and family life. But with it, where there is a will there is a way.

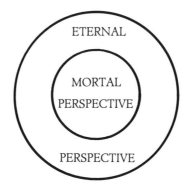

The accompanying simple diagram attempts to show two basic approaches in dealing with marriage and family life, a mortal one and an eternal one. The world generally teaches and understands the mortal. The restored gospel of Jesus Christ alone gives us the eternal. Secular (non-gospel-oriented) marriage and family counseling at best gives us only the best of the mortal, but it falls far short of the eternal.

Without question, the most overwhelming mortal problem we face is our mortal thought process itself. It bogs us down and leaves us attempting to lift ourselves by our own bootstraps. Such a mortal perspective becomes the cause of innumerable problems. As children of God, we are all eternal beings. Although our environment here is mortal, our challenges and decisions are of eternal consequence. An attempt to satisfy immortal challenges with mortal solutions is analogous to playing golf with a tennis racket: the tool is not suited to the reality. The thought process is not geared to the nature of the problem we are thinking about. To an animal, the holy scriptures are but an obstacle in a path, like another rock; similarly, to one possessing a mortal perspective alone, a relationship problem in the marriage or the family is another frustrating obstacle on a self-fulfillment path.

This idea can be illustrated easily in a simple experiment. Take a piece of paper and write at the top on the left side, "Mortal Perspective," and at the top on the right side, "Eternal Perspective." In the center of the page, make a list in abbreviated form of the relevant issues, concerns, or questions you have pertaining to marriage and family. Then make an effort to empathize with the two frames of reference, examining each issue or concern or problem in turn. Start with the mortal and attempt to divorce yourself from eternal understanding. Then move on to the eternal, which, as our diagram depicts, includes the mortal as well. The difference is critical—you don't have to divorce yourself from mortal understanding.

For instance, take the current burning issue of the role of man and woman and go through the above-described process. Remember, the mortal does not include the eternal, but the eternal does include the mortal. The eternal doesn't deny everyday realities of life, is not naive about powerful cultural forces at work in life, and doesn't ignore human tendencies and instincts. It not only embraces them all but goes far beyond them into understanding divine purposes, processes, and principles, and through sacred ordinances it cultivates the capacity, through spiritual promptings, to inspire appropriate practices in light of *both* eternal and mortal realities.

But such is not the case with the mortal frame of reference itself. It is ignorant of, thereby unconsciously ignores, the eternal perspective and realities. As examples of this, look at the responses the world gives to other front-burner issues concerning people today—economic matters, child discipline questions, in-law relationships, birth control, moral practices, life-style, problem-solving strategies, and so on.

The Challenge: Bridging the Ideal and the Real

However, there is a common problem in *only* focusing on the ideal, in staying alone in the outer circle and ignoring the inner one. A false dichotomy can be set up. A dichotomy means either/ or. Its fault is that it doesn't reflect the full reality. When people separate the abstract and the concrete, the ideal and the real, many end up frustrated. Although they may be temporarily "psyched," even inspired, by a description of the ideal, they come to see themselves as falling terribly short of it; in their mind the distance between the ideal and their own performance is so great that they feel the ideal to be an unreachable goal for them, that in a fundamental way they are incapable of attaining it. Alternatively, if they do not feel capable of it, they do not perceive what are the first steps they must take to attain it. This frustration can lead to a sense of increasing failure, futility, and hopelessness, and may eventually result in despair and depression.

To effectively reach people, you must reach them where they live—that is, in the practical everyday realities of ordinary life.

In the many years during which Truman Madsen and I have taught in various Education Weeks for Brigham Young University, we have seen the hurtful effects when the ideal and the real are not integrated or bridged by either the teachers or the patrons. When this bridge is not made, it is as if the person is living in two compartments of life—an abstract, ethereal, idealistic, spiritual one, and the mundane, gritty one of everyday life. If all things are truly spiritual to the Lord, as he reveals to us in modern revelation (D&C 29:34), and if we are to develop such a mind, then this artificial compartmentalization must be broken down. A bridge from the ideal to the real must be built. Constant integration of so-called sacred and secular material must be attempted if we are to have any real integrity.

This book is designed to serve that end.

Our Scripts
Come from People,
Not from Principles

Our childhood experiences can be very significant in the shaping of our lives. At that time we are most dependent, most vulnerable, and most needful of love, acceptance, and belonging. Our parents and significant others are our role models, the source of most of our satisfactions. We identify with these models, good or bad, not so much intellectually as emotionally. These experiences, positive and negative, have the cumulative effect of giving to us a life script. We normally think of a script as an actor's written part which he learns, memorizes, and acts out on stage. It not only involves his words and actions but also his attitude or frame of mind, his character. It becomes his part, his role.

All of us have scripts given to us which become our parts, our roles. I emphasize again that these scripts are more emotional, more subtly absorbed than they are intellectually or consciously chosen. They rise out of our deep vulnerabilities, our deep dependency upon others, and our absolutely screaming needs for acceptance and love, for belonging, for a sense of importance and worth, for a feeling that we matter.

All of this does not mean we are necessarily controlled by these scripts, but it does mean we are powerfully influenced by them. The difference between being influenced by and being determined by is 180 degrees. Determinism, whether it be genetic, psychic, or environmental, is false doctrine. It denies the power of the gospel. It is anti-Christ. In one sense the underlying assumption and tone of this entire volume is self-determinism, that we can learn to write our own scripts, that we can re-script ourselves, that we can identify with new models, have new relationships with true scripts, true models—divine ones. Just consider the word *scripture* itself. In the gospel context, is not one possible meaning "true scripts"?

However, in spite of the gospel, scripts written and developed early in life, pounded in by powerful emotional experiences—even traumatic ones—become deeply imbedded within our natures; and they may have influence upon us for the rest of our lives unless equally powerful, even traumatic, experiences divinely erase them and write new ones in the "fleshy tables of the heart." This is why those first eight years of life are so critical, so supremely important. This is why the role modeling of parents to children is their most basic, their most sacred, their most spiritual responsibility. Perhaps we could call it their highest Church calling. They are handing life's scripts to their children, scripts which in all likelihood will be acted out for much of the rest of the children's lives.

As parents, we may attempt to undo or even compensate for bad modeling by attempting to verbally teach correct principles. But principles are abstractions, and unless they are concretely internalized in our modeling (behavioral teaching) they simply will not take. What people identify with far more than what they hear is what they see and what they feel. If what they hear is in harmony with what they see and feel, it will then reinforce that observation and feeling. It will also give a verbal handle on how correct the concept is and why it works. The next generation will then also be able to teach by precept as well as by example, for they will be consciously competent to do so.

Becoming Consciously Competent

The accompanying little diagram shows the two pathways we can take to achieve a level of conscious competence, beginning from a position of unconscious incompetence.

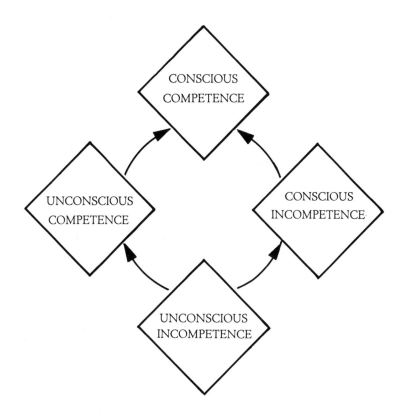

The unconsciously incompetent person simply is one who knows no better. He is a blunderer and doesn't know it. He simply thinks that's the way things are, that's the way people are, that's the way he is. He doesn't even attempt to question whether what he does is effective or not; he just does it. He lives out a script or program given to him; it fails, it's ineffective, it doesn't work, but these are not issues for him at all. He's unconsciously incompetent.

The person at the top of the diagram is consciously competent; he knows it works and he knows why it works, so he can continue to duplicate the process and follow the correct principles. He also can teach others the correct principles by precept as well as by example.

The one on the left is unconsciously competent. He is effective but doesn't know why he is effective. Perhaps he never questions why. He's also not sure how to improve—what to drop, what to keep. He can teach by example but not by precept. When he attempts to teach by precept, he can only read his autobiography. He doesn't know why it works, or that it has more to do with a mindset and an intricate set of principles or a philosophy than it does with practices. This can easily be observed when other people try to carry out the same practices; they don't work, because the people have changed only their practices, not their minds.

The consciously incompetent person on the right is usually just plain lazy. He knows that it isn't working and why it isn't working, but he doesn't have the internal desire or discipline, or both, to apply what he knows.

In helping any one of these four individuals, we would need to adapt our approach to the position he is in. Interestingly, it is usually the consciously competent people who read the books and attend the seminars, who choose to be actively involved in improving themselves in order to become better spouses and parents. They are the ones who really need it the least but benefit the most. They benefit in that they find reinforcement to continue to live the correct principles that have already made them successful.

I suggest the issue of humility is another independent variable in this discussion and that just as an unconsciously competent person could be humble or not, so could a consciously competent person. The Savior is the best example of humility in the latter type of person.

We Teach by Modeling

Oh, how surpassingly important it is for us as parents to realize that our day-to-day modeling is far and away our highest form of influence! We must not be like flying fish who occasionally shimmer beautifully in the sunlight. We must not hold forth eloquently on gospel principles and then plow back into the deep, where we spend most of our lives as grouches, as critics, as unfeeling, unloving people.

Principles don't love—people do. Neither do principles hate or reject or humiliate or belittle. Only people do these negative things. Without a doubt, the most powerful scripture most people ever read which becomes true for them, is the quality of the personal lives of those they need so badly.

Correct principles cannot and never will compensate for incorrect modeling, for bad examples. Never.

Perhaps the only principle we can model better than the Savior is repentance. When children sense parents turning back to the Lord and see them "confessing and forsaking" errors and wrongdoing, they are witnessing the divine growth process. Parents are thereby "allowed" to change and to grow, and children, seeing the process and the results, learn to build their ultimate trust and security in him who is perfect and "changeth not."

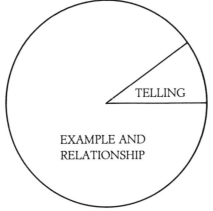

TELLING

EXAMPLE AND
RELATIONSHIP

I sincerely believe, without hyperbole, without exaggerating for effect, that scripting is about 90 to 95 percent example and relationship and 5 to 10 percent telling. The accompanying diagram represents this graphically.

The same proportions hold for divine scripting, as we will explore in depth as we go along. Divine scripts won't come from merely reading correct principles in the scriptures, but from identifying with and relating to the persons who live them, particularly with each member of the Godhead. The Savior was very clear and forceful and explicit on this when he chastened the Pharisees: "Search the scriptures; for in them *ye think* ye have eternal life; and they are they which testify of me. And ye will not come to me, that ye might have life." (John 5:39-40. Italics added.) Most people have only quoted verse 39, as if the Savior were encouraging people to search the scriptures—which of course we should do. But verse 40 gives the correct intent behind the Savior's expression. The purpose of the scripture search should be to come to Christ, to follow him, to feel his love and to love him, to identify with him emotionally as well as spiritually. In short, scripts come from people, not principles. "It is in the nature of plucked flowers to wither." Pull the principle away from its source, from an exemplar, and it will become dead, a correct abstraction.

As in all things, again the Savior is our model. He taught that he is the true vine, we are the branches, and the Father is the husbandman (John 15:1, 5). Such a magnificent metaphor unquestionably implies a relationship to a person. Our need for love is so great, and the Lord's capacity to give love is so great, that that is exactly the point where the binding, or the grafting, takes place; and the fruit inevitably follows.

Consider again the Savior's words:

"Abide in me and I in you. As the branch cannot bear fruit of itself, except it abide in the vine; no more can ye, except ye abide in me. I am the vine, ye are the branches. He that abideth in me, and I in him, the same bringeth forth much fruit; for without me ye can do nothing." (John 15:4-5.)

Going on, the Savior taught: "As the Father hath loved me, so have I loved you; continue ye in my love. If ye keep my commandments, ye shall abide in my love; even as I have kept my Father's commandments; and abide in his love." (John 15:9-10.)

Then the Savior gave his reason for teaching these things: "These things have I spoken unto you, that my joy might remain in you, and that your joy might be full" (John 15:11). True joy comes from within. It comes from the divine relationship nurtured by our keeping the commandments. It is not based on the external environment.

Then the Savior taught us to be loving models, as he has been to us. "This is my commandment, That ye love one another, as I have loved you" (John 15:12).

I find this idea that scripts come from people, not from principles, to be both thrilling and threatening. It's thrilling because I can do something about it; threatening because it's so much easier to verbally teach correct principles than to live them. It's so much easier to describe the mote in my children's lives than to deal with the beam in my own; so much easier to confess other people's sins than my own; so much easier to verbally teach correct principles to my students than it is to know and love them; so much easier to give brilliant tidbits of gospel advice to counselees than to empathize with them and also be open to them so that they can know and love me; so much easier to live independently than to live interdependently; so much easier to be a judge than to be a light; to be a critic than to be a model.

Conflicting Role Expectations

Now let's turn to the problems people face in marriage. I suggest that if you will examine them carefully, particularly their basic roots, you will find that in almost every case they arise out of conflicting role expectations, which is simply another way of saying script conflicts. For instance, the husband may think it is the wife's role to take care of the garden—his mother did. And the wife may think that is her husband's role, since her father did.

This may not be that big of a problem until they attempt to

solve it, and then their problem-solving scripts come to the surface. He is a passive aggressive: he slowly boils inside and says nothing but is judging continuously and becoming increasingly irritated. She is an active aggressive: she wants to talk it out, thrash it out, fight it out. She may yell and scream, or cry. They are in a state of collusion with each other, each needing the weakness of the other to validate his/her own perception and justify himself/herself. Each blames the other in his own way.

In this way a small problem becomes a large one, a molehill becomes a mountain. It may even become a mountain range, because conflicting problem-solving scripts simply compound every problem, magnify every difference. The whole thing becomes completely disproportionate.

Study your own marriage challenges and problems to see if they, too, are not fundamentally rooted in conflicting role expectations and compounded by conflicting problem-solving scripts.

Value/Goal Conflicts

In addition to scripts involving role-expectation conflicts or differences, there are conflicting scripts in two other closely related areas. First, values and goals, or the way things should be; and second, assumptions about the way things are. These two areas are closely interrelated, since we usually define the way things are in terms of the way things should be. For instance, when we say we have a problem we are basically saying things are not the way they should be. That is the definition of a problem. To one spouse the problem may be tragic; to the other, nonexistent.

Scripts regarding the way things should be (roles or goals) usually carry a great deal more emotional feeling. Scripts regarding the way things are are seldom questioned but they nevertheless underlie most misunderstandings and so-called communication breakdowns.

For instance, one spouse may think of the family as a so-called nuclear family or a two-generation family, while to the other spouse the concept of family is that it is intergenerational, and that spouse wants a great deal of open communication, inter-action, and activity with aunts and uncles, nieces and nephews, grandparents, and so forth.

One person may be scripted into believing that love is a feeling, while another person sees love as a verb and a fruit of the Spirit. To one, the Savior is an unknowable mystery; to another, he's our elder brother and perfect model. One may see the Church separate from the family; the other may see the family as the foundation of the Church and see the ward as scaffolding, the purpose of which is to build the family. One may think it impor-tant to separate the secular and the sacred; to the other, such compartmentalization is artificial. One may see a person as an intelligent animal; another, as a child of God with godlike poten-tial. One may believe in genetic and cultural determinism as a fact of life; another, in self-determinism. One may solve problems by fighting or flighting; the other wants to communicate and talk them through. One may see differences as weaknesses; the other may see differences as strengths. Where people stand on these issues will tend to be a product of their experiences with the significant models of their lives. They become their scripts.

Four Divine Scripting Models

The Lord does not leave us alone in these matters, completely dependent on earthly role models. He has provided divine models and describes them in the scriptures (true scripts). Consider four: first, Christ our Savior; second, his church or earthly kingdom; third, his home—the temple; and fourth, his creation, particularly the body. Let's consider each in turn.

Jesus Christ

Christ is our Savior and Redeemer, our elder brother, and he showed us the way to become like our Father in Heaven. ("I am the way.") He himself became like the Father, and he testified in many places that we, too, can do it by following him. When we are obedient to the laws and ordinances of the gospel with genuine intent and stay true and faithful to our covenants, we become increasingly like him and our Heavenly Father. And through the Holy Ghost they become mentors and trainers for us, giving us inspiration and guidance in all things. A mentor implies a relationship, one who watches over you, who cares about you, cares about your progress and development.

Through the gospel, Christ is also the father of the second birth. He becomes the father of our minds, as Elohim our Eternal Father is the father of our spirit bodies and our earthly parents are the parents of our physical bodies. When we enter into the covenant gospel through the waters of baptism, we take upon ourselves the name of Christ. Then it is as if we belong to a new family; we have a new childhood, a new early home life, new training, teaching, counseling, coaching, guiding.

The Church

The Church is a divine model organization. We become a member of the Lord's family, his church and kingdom, and a participant in assisting to bring to pass the immortality and eternal life of our Heavenly Father's other children, which is the Lord's work and glory. The Church is organized on a basis of stewardship principles. Correct principles are taught in the form of purposes and guidelines so that we can govern ourselves. Information, communication, problem-solving, and training systems are established to help Church workers magnify their stewardships and to coordinate and direct the work of the kingdom. The Church with its structure and systems and purposes and principles becomes an excellent organizational model for family living.

The Temple

The temple is a model home. The temple is the Lord's house. It is governed by heavenly principles of order, purpose, reverence, love, law, covenant making, and so on.

The next time you go to the temple, listen with your eyes to the sounds of a model home. Notice how clean, orderly, and purposeful everything is. Observe the sequence of preparatory ordinances, visual lecture presentations, covenants, and tests of knowledge, as a model for teaching. Study how each covenant builds on the earlier one, how understanding precedes covenanting, how progress flows out of obedience, how vital are unity, harmony, and love. Did you ever see an unkept room or hear people yell at each other in the temple?

The purpose of the temple is to develop eternal families through giving and binding us by covenant to divine laws and scripts, scripts of what our true goals and roles should be, as well as scripts of the way things really are. "Truth is *knowledge of* things as they are, and as they were, and as they are to come." (D&C 93:24. Italics added.)

Physical Creation

Apart from the above three acquired or adopted scripting models of spiritual processes, we are all born into another divine scripting model—physical creation, sometimes called nature. The human body is God's finest physical masterpiece. The body is considered to be a temple of God, as is the home; and if we are careful in our worship in the Lord's house, the temple, we learn the basic principles of conducting ourselves in the other two temples—the body and the home. We learn that the growth and development processes are lawful, that there is no shortcut, that everything is based upon correct principles, and that only through obedience to natural or divine law, with patience, faithful persistence, and diligence in obeying correct principles, can we optimize our growth and happiness. (Similarly, in the realm of science and technology, it is only when we obey the laws of nature that science has discovered that we can enjoy the fruits of modern technology.)

All things physical are made to bear witness of things spiritual, and people who have eyes to see and ears to hear and hearts to understand will comprehend these things and find a testimony of God himself—in all his creations. Again, to acquire such a mindset we must continuously "feast, not nibble" on the words of Christ and prayerfully search and ponder the scriptures, the source of true scripts.

I believe the body is the most powerful mortal teaching instrument we have. It is concrete, not an abstraction; it is always with us; we cannot violate it with impunity; we cannot feign strength we do not have; there is no shortcut to its development; it is the house of the spirit body; without physical health we are at best restricted in what we can do.

To obtain a body and train it to be subordinate to its spirit, and to train that spirit to be subordinate to the Spirit of the Lord, is the central purpose of mortality. Christ himself took on an earthly body and grew up as we do. The Church teaches us to respect our body, to obey the laws of health—mental, spiritual, emotional, and physical. The temple teaches us to reverence our body. In the resurrection we will have glorified, perfected bodies at the level of the law we lived in mortality, whether it be telestial, terrestrial, or celestial. (Study D&C 88:20-32.)

Two Goals:
P and PC

Fr* rom the study of all nature, particularly of the body, there
is one powerful lesson or script of transcendent importance to
marriage and family life. Simply put, it is this: In our efforts to get
what we want, we must preserve and enhance the asset or
resource which enables us to do this. As a form of shorthand
communication, I call these two goals P and PC. P stands for the
production of desired results; PC, for production capability,
which basically means the preservation and enhancement of the
results-producing assets or resources. I suggest this is an implicit
common denominator in all four divine scripting models.

To illustrate, what if we had a machine, and in an effort to
increase its productivity (P) we sped it up, ran it night and day,
and neglected proper maintenance (PC) activities? Sooner or later
it would break down, and production would decrease, but for a
while production, or P, would increase and outside observers
might be very impressed. Promotions might even be given as a
result. But eventually the chickens would come home to roost.

The machine would break down and production would stop, and the one then in charge might be blamed for it.

Now let's consider the body. How many of us have a health regimen of proper exercise, sound nutrition, and good stress management, with sufficient rest, relaxation, and recreation? On the other hand, how many of us neglect the body, exercise inconsistently, overeat, attempt to burn the candle at both ends? Perhaps for a while we can follow such a life-style, but eventually, for lack of PC, we will reap as we sow and P will nosedive; for the law of the harvest will always carry the future. Our energy level will drop in the afternoon and evening; we won't sleep as well; we'll become more easily irritable, moody; our self-esteem will decrease; and all of this will have a negative effect on our relationships with others. Many studies reported in the self-esteem literature conclude that about one-third of a person's self-esteem is a function of how he feels about his body.

Now let's apply the P/PC concept to marriage and family life. In this connection, let's use the metaphor of an emotional bank account. A financial bank account is one in which we make deposits from income sources and from which we withdraw for expense purposes. When we are financially overdrawn, we can make no more withdrawals without incurring debt. Similarly, an emotional bank account reflects the amount of deposits and withdrawals we have made over a period of time. If we have $100,000 in the emotional bank account, this gives us a great deal of flexibility and reserve and we can make withdrawals and make mistakes from time to time without jeopardizing this reserve, so long as the withdrawals are not too large or too many.

Consider a specific case. Let's say a parent has neglected PC work with a teenage son and gradually has developed an overdrawn emotional bank account. This means that the trust level is so low and the communication process so closed, mechanical, and unsatisfying to both that the son simply will not be open to the father's counsel on a matter requiring more experience and wisdom than the boy possesses. The father may have such wisdom and greatly desire to counsel his son, but the son will not open himself to it because of the overdrawn bank account. The P work, or the production of the desired results, will now suffer terribly, because the PC work has not been done. So the son may end up making decisions on a short-range emotional perspective, which may well result in many negative long-range consequences.

The father may sense all of this and desire to right the wrong of the past. He may make a few deposits in the form of showing interest in the son, paying attention, treating him with kindness and respect and consideration. But let's assume that the emotional bank account was $100,000 overdrawn and that these recent repentant deposits totalled $10,000. Let's also say that the issue was a fairly tender one, requiring $50,000 plus in the bank account before the son would feel sufficiently safe to open up regarding it, or to be open to the counsel given. The father still has $140,000 in deposits to make, but he will probably grow weary and impatient ("pulling up the flowers to see how the roots are coming") Then, in some kind of an irate, overreactive mood, he may belittle his son by calling him foolish in rejecting his recent kindnesses and counsel; and in this way he will withdraw, say, another $20,000, making himself now overdrawn or in debt by $110,000.

Unconditional Love

Once I had a stake president friend whose son didn't want to go on a mission. This terribly concerned his father, who wanted his son to be a model to the stake as well as to have and give the blessings of missionary work. The father pleaded and urged and talked. He also tried to listen to the boy to understand him, all the while in the hope that the son would turn about and agree to go on a mission.

The subtle message being communicated, I felt, was one of conditional love. The son felt that in a sense the father's desire for him to go on a mission outweighed the value he placed on him as a person and a son, and this, perhaps subconsciously, was terribly threatening (overdrawn emotional bank account). It stirred up a fight for the son's own identity and integrity, and he increased in his resolve not to go on a mission and to rationalize it away.

One day the father was strongly counseled to make within himself a sacrifice—a renunciation of conditional love; that he come to terms and make peace with the idea that his son might choose not to go on a mission; and that he should love his son unconditionally regardless of the latter's choice. Also, that his wife should do the same, and that they should both do what was necessary within their hearts and minds to make such a sacrifice. It was an extremely difficult thing to do, because for years they had planned on this mission. They had talked constantly about it. The boy had planned on it. He had even saved money for it in earlier years, but his interest had waned.

Now the father and mother went through a very difficult process of fasting and prayer and scripture study and, above all, the struggle to understand the nature of the unconditional love manifested in the atonement of Jesus Christ. Little by little they received more and more of the spirit of unconditional love, until they were deeply confirmed within themselves that they had not loved their son unconditionally but were now beginning to feel that love and wanted to express it. Then they communicated to the boy what they were doing and why, and told him they had come to the point at which they could say to him in honesty that whether he chose to go on a mission or not, it would not affect their complete feeling of unconditional love toward him. They didn't do this to manipulate the son, to try to get him to "shape up." They did it as the logical extension of their spiritual growth and character.

The son didn't give much of a response at the time, but the parents were in such a frame of mind now that it would have made no difference to their feelings for him. About a week later, the son told his parents that he had prayerfully considered the matter and had decided not to go on a mission. While they would have been very happy if he had said instead that he would go, the parents were perfectly prepared for this response and they continued to show unconditional love for him. Now everything was settled and life went along normally.

One day the son was sitting in a large assembly room at Brigham Young University, listening to one of the General Authorities give a devotional speech, when he felt the Spirit come upon him. It flooded his mind and heart with the desire to serve a mission. The next thing his stake president father knew was the son coming in for an interview to go off on a mission, following his interview with his bishop. Again the father showed by his unconditional love that he fully accepted the son's decision. The son said that he realized that, that that very realization had freed him from the unconscious or conscious fear of being pressured to serve a mission. Now that he had felt the Spirit inspire him to go on a mission, he really wanted to go with all his heart. His father was thrilled and happy, but he wasn't excessively elated, because he had truly sacrificed and had gone the second mile in a unique and creative way of showing love. And this had given him a deep sense of peace.

No Shortcut

There are many other ways of going the second mile, of making emotional deposits. Every situation is different. While the principle behind the emotional bank account is universal, what may be a deposit to one person may be a withdrawal for another. "What's one man's dessert is another man's poison." When we live the primary laws of love (PC activity) we encourage obedience to the primary laws of life (P results). There is no shortcut.

So also with the body. If we are out of shape and overweight, we must pay the price, the complete price. Cheap crash diets won't work; they only temporarily take off some water weight and lean muscle tissue and make us temporarily feel good—that is, "martyred-out" instead of "grossed-out." But sooner or later the "cheap grace" approach to physical salvation will reveal itself for what it is—a temporary but completely insufficient solution to a life-style problem. Similarly, in developing a celestial marriage or family culture, shortcut techniques, artificial rewards, psych-up strategies, duplicitous, hypocritical living—these may temporarily hide or mask the flawed structure, rotting beams, and sandy foundation, but those flaws will be exposed in the next storm of life.

President David O. McKay was one of the great husband/father models of the Church, and he frequently spoke of marriage as an eternal courtship requiring continual deposits in the form of gentleness, kindness, consideration, small courtesies, pleasant words, and unconditional love.

Any time we neglect PC in the name of P we may temporarily get a little more P, but eventually it will decline. If we use manipulative and intimidating techniques we can often get what we want in the short run, but eventually it affects the trust level, communication processes deteriorate, and a cynical culture is developed. In this climate, marriage relationships deteriorate. Instead of a rich, spontaneous understanding in which the two can communicate almost without words, in which they can even make mistakes in communication and the other partner will still get the meaning—instead of this the situation becomes one of mere accommodation wherein they simply attempt to live independent life-styles in a fairly respectful and tolerant way. It may further deteriorate to one of hostility and defensiveness in which a person is made an "offender for a word" and it's simply too risky to think out loud. These marriages may end up in open warfare in the courts or in a cold war at home, sustained only by children, sex, social pressure, or image projection.

Withdrawals and Deposits

One of the main differences between financial and emotional bank accounts is that emotional bank accounts are more fragile. They evaporate unless they continuously receive deposits. The absence of such deposits is tantamount to extreme love withdrawals. However, the good news in comparing financial and emotional bank accounts is the far greater amount of interest earned in the emotional one when deposits are being continually made. As the saying goes, "Love is the only thing which multiplies when we give it away." In a magnificent modern revelation, the Lord tells us exactly what the nature of the emotional bank account is and how deposits and withdrawals are made. President Stephen L Richards once called this revelation (D&C 121:34-36) a divine constitution of human relations.

Let's first look at the short-term (P) mentality in the withdrawal process.

. . . When we undertake to cover our sins, or to gratify our pride, our vain ambition, or to exercise control or dominion or compulsion upon the souls of the children of men, in any degree of unrighteousness, behold, the heavens withdraw themselves; the Spirit of the Lord is grieved; and when it is withdrawn, Amen to the priesthood or the authority of that man.

Behold, ere he is aware, he is left unto himself, to kick against the pricks, to persecute the saints, and to fight against God.

Now just as carefully attend to every phrase describing what PC deposits are like:

No power or influence can or ought to be maintained by virtue of the priesthood, only by persuasion, by long-suffering, by gentleness and meekness, and by love unfeigned;

By kindness, and pure knowledge, which shall greatly enlarge the soul without hypocrisy, and without guile—

Reproving betimes with sharpness, when moved upon by the Holy Ghost; and then showing forth afterwards an increase of love toward him whom thou hast reproved, lest he esteem thee to be his enemy;

That he may know that thy faithfulness is stronger than the cords of death. (D&C 121:37-38, 41-44.)

We must simply not allow ourselves to become too P-oriented, or for that matter too PC-oriented. As in everything else, the key is *balance.* Let us again clarify what this means. P, or the production of desired results, is the equivalent of having a clean house or a clean room. PC, or production capability, means that those who are responsible to clean that house or room will do so cheerfully without being reminded. In other words, they will be committed up front to their responsibility and will be so reinforced by the emotional bank account that they are internally motivated to do their jobs with initiative and cheerful diligence.

Of course, you can get P, or the production of a clean room, by yelling and nagging and threatening and wielding the carrot and the stick, but in the process you will be draining the emotional bank account, so that when you are away, not present to nag and cajole and threaten and so forth, the room will simply not be cleaned. And when you do nag, the room will be done grudgingly, in a slovenly and only a mediocre way. Such nagging will also contribute to the corruption of the child's conscience, wherein "the wrong is in getting caught," not in doing wrong—such as not keeping a commitment.

We could multiply these illustrations almost endlessly and see again and again that when we go for P in a way which undermines PC—that is, the emotional bank account, the up-front commitment on what the desired results are, and the guidelines to work with them—we will simply not maintain P, or production, over time. As the revelation puts it, "No power or influence can . . . be maintained." Power and influence in this context may by synonymous. We simply cannot maintain influence with people over time except upon the principles of righteousness.

When we discuss four basic systems which parents need to set up and manage, we will look further at the twin goals of P and PC in order to obtain a deeper practical understanding.

Suffice it to say here that the P/PC principle is applicable to literally every asset and resource we use to accomplish anything —our body, our mind, our emotional power, our spirituality, and our relationships. In business it would apply to every human resource, including customers, employees, managers, owners, suppliers, distributors, and the public generally. If the P/PC principle is thrown out of balance in either direction, it will have a domino effect and negatively reverberate through every other resource.

We all have 168 hours in every week, and I suggest at least 3 hours should be spent in PC on the body in exercise, 7 hours exercising the mind in reading and other personal and professional development activities, and 7 hours on the spirit in both private and public worship and study. I am convinced that such a private PC effort would significantly improve and increase the productivity, the satisfaction, the quality, and the effectiveness of every other hour of that entire week, including the depth and restfulness of one's sleep. (For most people, the only trade-off is lost TV time.)

If we truly spend 30 minutes a day with our Father in Heaven will we not be more likely to spend eternity with him?

19

Three Roles:
Producer, Manager,
and Leader

To accomplish the P/PC goals, spouses and parents play three roles: producer, manager, and leader. The *producer* does the things necessary to accomplish desired results, which we have called the P goal. For instance, a child who cleans his or her room is in the producer role. The parent who does the dishes or takes out the garbage or does the yardwork or puts the baby to bed is a producer. A producer may or may not use tools—such as a power lawnmower, a vacuum cleaner, or a dishwasher—to increase results.

The second vital role is the *manager* role. The manager sets up and works with and through people and systems. For instance, the parent may delegate various jobs around the home and the yard to the children, the parent playing the manager role and children the producer roles. This delegation has the effect of moving the fulcrum over. In the following two diagrams, the producer role represents a one-to-one relationship between input and output, so that if a person puts in one hour of effort, he will produce one unit of results. Ten hours of input will produce ten hours of results, assuming no loss of efficiency.

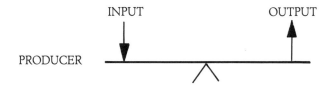

But this is not the case with the manager role. Through effective delegation (moving the fulcrum over), one unit of input could produce ten or fifty or a hundred units of productivity.

MANAGER

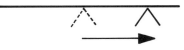

Management work is essentially the work of moving the fulcrum over, and is the key to any kind of significant organizational growth.

As a further clarification of this principle, consider the analogy of a teeter-totter. By moving the point of balance far enough to the right side, a small person seated on the left side could lift a large person seated on the right.

To use a business analogy, if you set up a sandwich shop and made and sold sandwiches, you would be a producer. If your sandwich shop became very popular and you decided to expand into a second shift, you would probably move into the manager role for that second shift, hiring a producer to make and sell the sandwiches. If, however, your customers complained that the sandwiches were inferior in quality to the ones you made on the day shift, you might possibly take over the second shift yourself and be a producer for two shifts. The net result, of course, would be a loss of health or family or both, with an eventual loss of business, because no one can work sixteen hours every day and properly maintain other values.

But this is exactly what happens with many producer parents. They don't know how to delegate, how to move the fulcrum over by working with and through others, so they end up doing the work themselves and killing themselves off. Thus many parents go to bed every night exhausted and often irritable and critical, disappointed that others are not being of more help.

The producers are usually good at producing. They like it. Abraham Maslow made a brilliant, far-reaching statement which explains in part the problem: "He that is good with a hammer tends to think everything is a nail." Producers think the solution to most problems is simply to put their hand to the plow and get the job done. That is why their operations stay small or why their businesses go under. They simply do not know how to delegate to other people. They would like to delegate, but they don't know how to do it well so that others are internally motivated and will follow through on expectations.

Most producers from time to time attempt to delegate, but they often end up saying, "It takes me more time to explain it and to train this person than to do it myself. Besides, every time I turn it over to someone else they don't do it nearly as well as they should, or at least, as well as I can." So they give up on the delegation process and go back to producing, and they end up bone-weary, self-pitying,. and martyred. They are forever overburdened, rushed, fatigued, and disappointed, and they lose faith in others in coming through. They are not managers; they don't think like managers. They are unaware of the importance of strategy, structure, and system; of how to get others internally committed through involvement in decision-making. They overreact to mistakes and move in quickly to correct them. They hover over and constantly check up, which in turn undermines the motivation of the delegatees and thereby fulfills the prophecy of the delegator: "I knew it; I knew they wouldn't come through. You just simply can't depend on others!"

Another reason they hesitate to do management work is that the time spent in moving the fulcrum over takes away from the many jobs to be done, and when those jobs are not done, things are worse than they were before. And the spouse or parent becomes more and more convinced that "the only way to get it done is to do it myself."

The strength of the producer is diligence, skill, knowledge, competence, and loyalty. The weakness of the producer is lack of leverage, not moving the fulcrum over, being completely tied to his own effort. The strength of the manager compensates for the weakness of the producer. He or she knows how to move the fulcrum over to get leverage so that many times the results are obtained with even less effort. The manager understands the need for organizational structure and for systems, particularly training, communication, information, and compensation. The manager also recognizes the need for certain uniform and standard procedures and practices based on correct principles, so that much of the production will be done while on automatic pilot, as it were.

The weakness of the manager is a tendency to be inflexible, to think like a bureaucrat, to lose vision, to become methods oriented and procedures oriented, to become systems minded. Most organizations lose sight of their essential mission within a few years of their establishment. They become methods focused rather than results focused. In other words, their objectives focus on methods rather than results. Such was the case with the railroad industry, which lost sight of its essential transportation function and instead saw itself in the railroading business. Then as it gave its energies to building better railroads, better railroad cars, better railways, more efficient engines, and so on, the pipelines, the airlines, and the truck lines took away most of the business. If we define effectiveness as being results minded and efficiency as being methods minded, over time managers tend to focus on efficiency, not on effectiveness—that is, on doing things right instead of doing the right things.

How is this problem to be solved? That is, what can compensate for the weakness of a manager? Certainly the producer can't. The producer thinks as an independent person. The producer is usually a loner, whereas a manager has to deal with the interdependent nature of team effort, such as in a marriage or a family or a business.

This analysis points up the necessity of another role, which we call the *leader* role. The leader's essential purpose is to provide direction through modeling and vision, to motivate through love and inspiration, and to build a complementary team based on mutual respect. A leader is effectiveness minded, not efficiency minded. A leader is constantly concerned with direction and results rather than with methods, systems, and procedures. A manager may climb the ladder and get to the top rung, but it would take a leader to indicate that the ladder was leaning against the wrong wall.

Above all, the leader possesses such vision and a sense of direction. While all of the producers are hacking their way through the jungle and their managers are sharpening their machetes for them and setting up machete-wielding working schedules and putting on training programs for machete wielders, a leader may cry out, "Wrong jungle!" But they all answer back: "Be quiet! We're making progress."

In other words, a leader learns how to stand apart as an observer and to ask basic questions about the methods, procedures, and systems being employed. A leader recognizes the continual need to adapt, to be flexible, to change. But since changes often upset people and disturb the culture, the leader must lubricate the processes of change so that they are acceptable to others. The leader does this through deposits into the emotional bank accounts made primarily from example and modeling, from warmth, love, kindness, consideration, and empathy, balanced with courage, drive, initiative, and resourcefulness.

The leader is the one who builds the complementary team so that the strength of the producer can be fully utilized and his weakness made irrelevant by the strength of the manager. And the weakness of the manager is compensated for by the strength of the leader. The leader doesn't attempt to clone people or to make everyone else over in his own image, but he realizes that as long as people have the same goals it is important that they have different roles. (Note that in the Godhead, the Father, the Son, and the Holy Ghost have the same goal, but each performs a different role.) The spirit of a complementary team is the spirit of mutual respect, so that differences are utilized and are considered strengths rather than weaknesses.

Oftentimes we see situations in which spouses or parents are good managers but poor leaders; that is, they have good logistical systems, everything is orderly and systematic, thought out carefully in advance, but the feeling isn't good; it's too officious, too formal, too efficient, too blatantly logical. A leader, on the other hand, compensates for this by providing an emotional climate of warmth and understanding and love so that others are internally motivated.

Frequently, also, we find many leaders who are poor managers, who possess motivational and directional qualities but lack skill in establishing and working through systems.

These three roles—the producer, the manager, and the leader—are all absolutely vital in family life and marriage. They are interdependent roles, even though they are separate. In the early stages of marriage both partners must play all three roles, perhaps with more emphasis on one than another, and as children come along and are capable of carrying more responsibility the manager and leader roles will tend to become increasingly important. Eventually, by the third generation if not before, the leader role becomes the most important for the parent or grandparent.

Now exactly how do these roles relate to the P/PC goals spoken of before? The producer role obviously is working directly on the P goal, on activities which produce desired results. The manager and the leader are focused upon PC or production capability; that is, they work with and through other people, using systems and procedures in order to produce the desired results. It is highly important that the manager and the leader realize that they are working on PC goals and that production of desired results, or P, comes about as the product of this PC activity. Otherwise, they may find themselves in the producer role, "in the wrong jungle," managing by crisis. This is exactly how many families are run. The best physical analogy I can think of is the pounding surf; one huge wave after another, one huge problem or crisis after another, with almost no space to catch one's breath. (Elder Paul H. Dunn once compared the role of a mission president to that of a Scoutmaster taking two hundred Boy Scouts on an overnight hike for two years.)

The accompanying diagram may help explain the relationship between the two goals and the three roles.

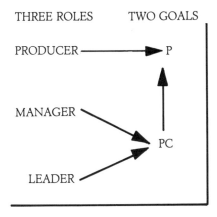

This diagram, of course, does not mean that managers and leaders should not also be producers. They should be producers of some things but not of all things. One of the characteristics of a true leader is that he sees himself as being no better than those he leads; therefore, he is not above doing their kind of work, including some "grunt work." He certainly cannot spend all or most of his time doing this work, or there will be no time for leadership, but the willing performance as a servant doing P work, as required from time to time, becomes part of the leader's activity. He also continually learns from feeling the pulse of those in the trenches. Such modelling inspires followership. The Savior taught that the greatest is he who is the servant of all (Matthew 20:27), but he also acknowledged that it is not reasonable that his apostles should "leave the word of God, and serve tables" (Acts

6:2). In other words, they are to stay in their sacred, spiritual ministries as servants of the people for God's cause rather than to leave them for temporal duties.

Perhaps it is important to emphasize again the relationship between P and PC. We could say that P is the child of PC; in other words, we train people so that they can be more productive. The manager sets up the training system for producers and the leader makes certain that the training system is going in the right direction, is based on correct principles, and is imbued with the correct spirit.

A parent who is P oriented would be like the one who only cares about a clean house or well-kept yard. He or she would do all of the work and would probably criticize the children for not doing their part. The children would be insufficiently trained and committed to do their part and, worst of all, the parents might have a well-kept house and yard but lose their children.

From my training experiences, I have found it to be an extremely helpful exercise, in the effort to teach the two goals and three roles, to have people use this as a kind of theory or conceptual scheme to figure out what is really happening in different family situations. I find that as people's abilities to diagnose what is happening increases, they can then take the appropriate steps to remedy the situations. But until the diagnosis is accurate, as in medicine, obviously any prescription or therapeutic action will be misapplied.

For instance, let's say you have an "at home" mother who is constantly in a producer role, a breadwinning father who attempts to play the manager role, no one playing the leader role, and the children doing little, if anything, and that grudgingly. It's apparent in this situation that both parents are neglecting the leader role, the mother is neglecting the manager role, and very little PC work is being done. Emotional bank accounts are probably overdrawn, and until mother cleans it up, the house will look as if a hurricane has gone through it almost daily.

In another situation, parents play the manager roles, but the children do poorly in the producing roles simply because the parents neglect the leader role and there isn't a good feeling present. The children are not internally motivated, they're not committed. In another instance, the parents play the leader role and neglect the management role, so that there are not well-established systems and procedures and, even though there is a good feeling present, everything is basically disorganized.

On the other hand, managers may organize exceptionally well, the house is clean and the yard well kept, but the more significant issues of life such as education, health, spirituality, and love may be neglected altogether. This is like "straightening deck chairs on the *Titanic*."

As an insight-producing exercise, consider these two goals and three roles and think them through with regard to your particular marriage and family situation. Do the same for the homes both the spouses came out of. You will probably discover how you were scripted and perceive your present goals and roles accordingly. Next consider the divine models we have spoken about—the Savior, the Church, the temple, and the physical creation, particularly the body—to learn better scripts, divine scripts, true scripts. Again, the scriptures would be your primary information source.

Then, when you realize you're free agents and are not determined by scripts given to you in your own upbringing, you can give yourself over to the divine rescripting process. If the partner or a child won't cooperate, the four models even teach how to react or respond to this: with correct principles, persuasion, longsuffering, kindness, and so on, rather than with judgment, condemnation, and accusation.

I enthusiastically encourage parents and families to consider these two goals and three roles as a useful way of figuring out what is going on, where the problems are, and how they should be corrected.

20

Brain Dominance Theory and the Three Roles

A great deal of research has been conducted for decades on what has come to be called brain dominance theory. The bottom line of the findings basically indicates that as the brain is divided into two hemispheres, the left and the right, each hemisphere tends to specialize in and preside over different functions, process different kinds of information, and deal with different kinds of problems. The left hemisphere is the more logical/verbal one and the right hemisphere the more intuitive, creative one.

While both hemispheres are involved in logical and creative processes, the left works more with logic, the right works more with emotions (self and others). The left deals with words, the right with pictures; the left with parts and specifics, the right with wholes and the relationship between the parts. The left deals with analysis, which means to break apart; the right with synthesis, which means to put together. The left deals with sequential thinking— one, two, three, four, five, and so forth; the right with simultaneous and holistic thinking. The left is time bound, meaning it has a sense of time and goals and one's position in relation to those goals; the right is time free, in that the person could lose altogether a sense of time. The left governs the right side of the body, and the right, the left side of the body. (Studies have shown that brain dominance is not necessarily related to handedness; the above thinking pertains to almost all of the right-handed people and over two-thirds of the left-handed people. For the remainder, the functions are reversed.)

Admittedly this description is a little oversimplified, and new scientific studies are being continually done and undoubtedly will throw more light on brain functioning. I personally believe that new scientific and revealed discoveries over the years will significantly change the way we think about how the brain works and will greatly amplify, and thereby eclipse, brain dominance theory. (It really makes no difference which side we're operating from when it comes to the point I'm trying to make.) The point is that the brain is capable of many, many different kinds of functions, and experts all agree on one thing: we are barely scratching the surface of our potential use of it. This would be analogous to a person with most of his or her muscles latent or dormant just awaiting development through exercise.

Using the theory, certainly we live in a very left-brain-dominant world, where words and measurement and logic are enthroned and the creative, more intuitive, sensing, artistic side is often subordinated, even punished. This is particularly true with men, where the male macho cultural stereotype combined with the heavy academic focus on the left side can often neglect or even drive out the more creative, aesthetic, intuitive capacities often considered the feminine side.

Applying brain dominance theory to the analysis of the three roles described above, the manager role would primarily be left brain and the leader role right brain. The producer role would depend upon the nature of the work being done. If it's verbal, logical, analytical work, that would be essentially left brain; if it's more intuitive, emotional, or creative work, it would be right brain.

This theory may help explain why some people could be excellent managers and poor leaders—primarily because they are left-brain dominant. And why others could be excellent leaders and poor managers—because they are right-brain dominant. Leadership involves motivation, and motivation is primarily right brain. We are not motivated by how we think; we are motivated by how strongly we feel about what we think. The person who speaks of himself as being logical, down-to-earth, and practical rather than acting and living on emotions, usually says it with passion!

In this sense excellent managers but poor leaders may be extremely well-organized with superior systems and procedures and with everyone clearly understanding their roles, with well-spelled-out job descriptions, and so on—a really tight ship. But the problem is that little gets done because they are not internally motivated. There is no feeling; there is no heart; everything is too mechanical, too formal, too tight, too protective. A looser organization may work much better even though it may appear to an outside observer to be disorganized and confused. Truly significant accomplishments result simply because the people in the organization share a common vision or sense of purpose—and this governs them. With a high trust level existing, the more subtle, informal forms of communication are the channels through which the work gets done. Such organizations, familial or industrial, have a unique internally motivating culture. The Japanese, as well as most of the outstanding companies in America, teach us a great deal about culture, leadership, the long view, craftsmanship, pride in work, cooperation, quality, internal motivation, and consensus decision making.

I believe these are the same characteristics of the great families in the scriptures. The prophets of God are, above all, visionary seers, are driven by divine purposes, and are motivated by, and motivate others by, a certain kind of love—a Christlike kind—"charity towards all men, and to the household of faith" (D&C 121:45).

Of course, the ideal is to cultivate and develop the ability to have good lateralization or crossover between the right and left sides of the brain so that a person could first sense or discern what the situation called for and then use the appropriate tool to deal with it. If someone were to ask you, speaking of chess, "What's the best move?" you'd first have to ask, "What's the situation?" Then you could decide what the best move would be. If someone were to ask you, "What is the best club to use in golf?" you'd first have to ask what the lay of the land was, where the hole was, what the score was, and so forth. The ability to correctly diagnose the situation is the first ability, and this itself may require a good combination of left and right brain.

The Eastern cultures speak of the two parts of man's nature, calling them the Yin and the Yang. The Yin is the feminine part and the Yang the masculine. Entire books have been written on this subject, even organizational books. Many organizations have great management systems and controls but lack heart. Others may have heart but lack mind, good systems, and controls. The ancient Greek philosophers spoke of influence or persuasion processes in terms of ethos, pathos, and logos—ethos basically having to do with establishing one's credibility, or what I have been calling the emotional bank account; pathos dealing with the emotional or motivational part, which we would here call the right brain; and logos dealing with the logical reasoning process, which we would here call the left brain.

Once while I was conducting a management training session in Orlando, Florida, on the subject of "Manage on the Left, Lead on the Right," the president of the company came to me during the morning break absolutely enthralled and fascinated by the subject. But he felt that it had particular relevance to his marriage and asked if I would have lunch with his wife and him at the noon break. I happily complied, and he requested that I simply observe the way they talked with each other.

The three of us sat together, and he explained to his wife a little bit of what I had taught that morning and that he had asked me to observe their communication in relation to the problems and challenges they faced in their marriage. She was more than anxious to cooperate. He started by acknowledging to her that he felt he should be more sensitive and considerate of her needs and asked her if she would mention a specific thing that he could do or change that would make her happy. She responded by saying that it wasn't a specific thing, it was more a general thing. She put it in this way: "It's more a sense I have about priorities. I just don't feel that marriage is as important to you as to me, or as you tell me it is to you."

He replied, "You keep telling me that, but I don't know what you mean. Give me something specific." (The left brain deals in parts and specifics.) He said he simply couldn't "deal with a sense about priorities." He said the marriage was very important to him in spite of what she thought, but that he couldn't go to work on proving it to her unless she would give him some specific things to do. "After all," he said, "haven't I given you everything you've wanted? Don't you live where you want to live, in the kind of house you want to live in? Don't you do the things you want to do and go where you want to go?"

He continued on like this until she became rather irritated and said, "You don't know what I'm saying at all. Those things are fine, but they're not what I'm talking about. What I mean is that I just don't feel as important in your life."

He responded, "There you go again about feelings."

She said, "Well, they are feelings."

He said, "That's the problem with you, honey, and that's the problem with your mother. In fact, it's the problem with almost every woman I know."

She said, "Well, it's hard to put it into words."

He looked on her and then me with almost utter disdain, as if to say, "How long can I endure this dumbness?" He said, "All day long I work with words and with facts and figures and things I can get a handle on. Now, honey, I really want to work on the marriage if you will just help me get a handle on specifically what I can do."

She continued in her line of communication and he in his, until little by little it was obvious to me that they were taking more and more deposits from the already overdrawn emotional bank accounts. I intervened, looked at him, and said, "Is this kind of how it goes?"

He sighed. "Every day."

I looked at her and all she said was, "It's the story of our marriage."

Here were two "half-brained" people trying to communicate with each other, unaware that the real strength of their marriage lay in its differences and that they literally needed each other's strengths and capacities to compensate for their own deficiencies and weaknesses. Instead they were like two ships passing each other at night, unaware of each other.

Remember Maslow?—"He that is good with a hammer tends to think everything is a nail." Those who are good with the left brain tend to think every kind of problem is amenable to left-brain processing; and vice versa. Most of the truly great breakthroughs in science have come with breakwiths—usually from right-brain philosopher/scientist/leader types who stand apart and ask basic questions and receive inspiration or hunches or intuition or insights or flashes which cause them to reconceptualize the whole situation (to shift paradigms). Pure science (hypothesis formation) is primarily right brain; applied science (hypotheses testing and using), based on the logical/scientific method, is more left brain. Hypothesis formation is far more significant than hypothesis testing in terms of long-term contribution to society, but both play a very important role, and one without the other is completely inadequate.

Comfort zone is a popular term that is coined for the purpose of describing where people feel most at home—maybe a physical comfort zone, or a social or psychological comfort zone. Left-brain people are very comfortable in left-brain environments with left-brain challenges, and very uncomfortable in right-brain environments with right-brain challenges. Some entire professions are primarily left brain, and my consulting experience has convinced me this is one of their major problems. They simply don't deal with the "leader" role in their firm or in their profession. They are often good professionals but poor business leaders. They spend too much time in the "wrong jungle."

We must learn to leave our comfort zones if we are going to develop other parts of our nature. The physical exercise credo is valid—"no pain, no gain." A person who is left-brain dominant should purposely exercise dormant right-brain muscles, including learning to communicate through sensing and touching and visual imagery and to listen more with the eyes than the ears, getting involved in artistic endeavors and the creative side of problem-solving, and so forth. Those who are right-brain dominant should exercise the latent left-brain muscles through analytical problem-solving processes, communication through words and logic, reading textbooks, studying scientific and technical material such as computer science, law, business accounting, and most of the applied sciences.

Rescripting Through Visualization

It might be that what in theology we call the heart (the higher, more godly attributes) represents the powers and capacities of the right side of the brain. One of the most powerful and effective ways of rescripting ourselves is to use the unique, right-side human endowment called the imagination. As vividly as possible we imagine or visualize ourselves following the divine scripts we are learning from the divine models. Many studies have shown and are showing the power of mental imagery, of visualizing correct behavior or goal achievement over and over again in a relaxed state of body and mind, seeing ourselves in our mind's eye in full sensory, three-dimensional detail—including feeling the satisfactions which would naturally result from such achievements.

There is a great deal of popular "success" literature which teaches the principle of constructive imagination, usually called visualization/affirmation. Much of this literature, I believe, is on the right track, but it falls far short of where the gospel would take us with these capacities. The gospel not only gives us celestial content, in the form of divine scripts for our visualization/affirmations, but also gives us celestial methodology to bring it off, including prayer and meditation and, most importantly, the ordinances of the gospel. Isn't it interesting that the Lord wants us in mortality to see ourselves going into his presence in a simulated reality in his sacred house? Many people are deeply scripted into believing they don't have celestial potential. When we partake of the sacrament, can we visualize taking upon ourselves the name of Christ and keeping his commandments? Can we visualize his atoning sacrifice, and ourselves being reconciled to God through receiving this atonement by our faith, repentance, and ordinances?

> "And now behold, I ask of you, my brethren of the church, have ye spiritually been born of God? Have ye received his image in your countenances? Have ye experienced this mighty change in your hearts?
>
> Do ye exercise faith in the redemption of him who created you? Do you look forward with an eye of faith, and view this mortal body raised in immortality, and this corruption raised in incorruption, to stand before God to be judged according to the deeds which have been done in the mortal body?
>
> I say unto you, can you imagine to yourselves that ye hear the voice of the Lord, saying unto you in that day: Come unto me ye blessed, for behold, your works have been the works of righteousness upon the face of the earth?" (Alma 5:14-16.)

This is the frequently taught scriptural concept of spiritual creation. It's a personal seership using the gift of the Holy Ghost, which was given "to bring all things to your remembrance" (John 15:26), to "guide you into all truth," and to "shew you things to come" (John 16:13). This would boggle the minds of the uninitiated, but it thrills those who are honest in heart and ready to receive. The PMA literature (Positive Mental Attitude) is like a pigmy when compared to the giant celestial literature. It's terrestrial at best. It's sad to see some "success-oriented" Church members gobble up popular self-improvement literature while they give little sustained, deep, prayerful, pondering attention to the celestial self-improvement/success literature sitting like "acres of diamonds" in their backyard.

I am not necessarily against this secular success literature; it serves some good purposes and teaches many correct principles. But it just barely scratches the surface of the powers that can be released through covenant making and ordinances. Perhaps the best principle it teaches is the principle of right-brain visualization, or the programming of the deeper mind by the conscious mind's using mental pictures or images. We should never be satisfied to operate by the light of the moon and the stars when we have available to us the light of the noonday sun, which enables us to see everything else.

Perhaps one reason why some faithful Church members haven't experienced the life-changing power of the ordinances, particularly of the sacrament and the temple, is that they are simply too left brained. Their main instrument of spiritual perception and understanding is shut down. Of course, the level of one's personal righteousness is a much more significant factor in attaining this life-changing power.

Anwar Sadat, past President of Egypt who was assassinated, took the bold peace initiative of going to Israel after swearing that he would "never shake the hand of an Israeli as long as they occupy one inch of Egyptian soil." He explained that he rescripted himself by learning how to reside variously in religious, meditative, or self-teaching states of mind. In his autobiography, referring to an early imprisonment, he described the experience:

> One of the things Cell 54 taught me was to value that inner success which alone maintains one's inward equilibrium and helps a man to be true to himself. . . . Once released from the narrow confine of "self" . . . a man will have stepped into a new, undiscovered world which is vaster and richer. . . . This is why I regard my last eight months in prison as the happiest period in my life. . . . Now that I had discovered and actually begun to live in that "new world," things began to change. My narrow self ceased to exist . . . in the world I came to experience friendship with God—the only friend who never lets you down or abandons you.

During this time Sadat formed the lifelong conviction that the source of permanent power is inner success:

> Most people are fascinated by outward success. . . . If their external image is, for any reason, shaken, they are inevitably shaken and may even collapse. . . . [But] outward success alienates a man from himself.

Sadat cultivated the habit of preparing himself for a state of creativity by letting go of old fears and suspicious, wornout ideas and methods. Here is his explanation of how he was able to vacate the emotional script that had made Israel taboo for his whole generation.

> It was then I drew, almost unconsciously, on the inner strength I had developed in Cell 54 of Cairo Central prison—a strength, call it a talent or capacity for change. . . . My contemplation of life and human nature in that secluded place had taught me that he who cannot change the very fabric of his thought will never, therefore, make any progress. The fact that change is a prerequisite of progress may be axiomatic; but the fact that change should take place first at a deeper and perhaps subtler level than the conscious level was one I had established as a basis of action ever since I discovered my real self in Cell 54. (Anwar Sadat, *In Search of Identity*, Harper and Row, 1978.)

Each of us can test the usefulness of spiritual creation. In a relaxed state of mind and heart, let's see ourselves, as clearly and vividly as possible, as spouses or parents following divine models and divine principles in our everyday lives, particularly in the difficult moments of stress, disappointment, fatigue, and frustration. Let's mentally rehearse our scripts. Let's do it before we encounter the day. Private victories precede public victories. Gethsemane preceded Calvary. Blueprints precede construction.

The world was created twice, first spiritually, second temporally.

Begin with the end in mind.

21

Three Bermuda Triangles

Bermuda Triangle means disaster. If any one of the three important roles is neglected—producing, managing, and leading —disaster will result.

First Bermuda Triangle: No Producer

How many of us have had great ideas and high resolve but simply did not come through? Disaster. The work simply doesn't get done. The rooms are not cleaned, the journals not written, the genealogical research not done, the party not given, the commitment not kept.

Second Bermuda Triangle: No Manager

Where there is no manager, everyone attempts to be a producer working independently, even though the very nature of the reality of marriage and family life is that it is interdependent. In this situation the wheel is being reinvented every day; there are no established systems and procedures which have worked well in the past. Everyone is exhausted from production. There is a great deal of role conflict and ambiguity; then when the work doesn't get done, people often accuse each other for the failure. They get into a blaming mode. They develop mote/beam sickness—"Why beholdest thou the speck of sawdust in thy wife's eye but considerest not the two-by-four plank in thine own?" And the people involved get into collusion with each other, wherein they literally need each other's weaknesses to validate their perception of each other and to justify their own lack of production.

Producers usually think independently in an interdependent situation. When the essence of the relationship requires a team spirit, cooperation, and interdependent thinking, independent production spells disaster.

It simply takes a great deal more maturity to go for interdependence than for independence. Of course, independence is a much more mature state than dependence and is a necessary but insufficient condition for interdependence. Much of the world's popular literature focuses upon achieving independence. Many of the popular movements of today again focus upon independence. Independence is a worthy thing to strive for, but it is not the *most* worthy goal. Thoroughly selfish people could be independent. Interdependent people must learn to communicate and cooperate, to give and take and synergize (going for better and better mutually beneficial solutions), to accommodate each other's interests, to gain understanding of each other's concerns, priorities, perceptions, and feelings. They must learn to adapt, to be flexible and patient, to control self, and to give of self.

That is why producers are often loners. A mountain man is a producer; he cherishes his independence, his self-reliance. But there's no deep personality growth, no moving the fulcrum over, no leverage. While God's kingdom is to be independent of all other creatures on earth (D&C 78:14), its work is based on interdependence, not on independence. By definition, Zion is a community of the "pure in heart," in which each puts the interests of others ahead of his own.

However, you can never do calculus without understanding algebra. Similarly, you can never have the skills and attitudes of interdependence without the skills and attitudes of independence. We don't move from dependency to interdependency. We must go through independency. People who are not in charge of themselves, who are unable to guide and direct their own lives toward their own goals, will not be equipped to manage and lead others and to learn to give and take, cooperate, and communicate. A person who is emotionally dependent upon another cannot be interdependent with the other because he lacks sufficient possession of himself. He lacks courage to give necessary feedback, to call it as he sees it, to represent himself, his views and convictions. He will tend to become either a clone or a rebel, both of which are forms of dependence, the former a positive dependence and the latter a counterdependence. Both forms demonstrate that the person is being controlled.

Often teenagers get into a counterdependency with their parents, wherein they do the actual opposite of what the parents want. Parents often interpret this rebellion as evidence that they have lost influence and control. In one sense this is true, but in another sense they are still in control and possess influence, but in a negative way. In early stages of immaturity the love-hate relationship or the fight-flight problem-solving strategies are good illustrations of people who are in a counterdependency and acting as if they were independent. Parents should be very wise and see the situation as it really is and not overreact or give up on themselves, but simply hang in, rolling with the punches, smiling a lot, loving unconditionally. They should symbolically write these kinds of affirmations on walls, mirrors, forearms, and hearts: "Steady as she goes." "This, too, shall pass." "Don't take it personally." "Roll with the punches." They will find that if they continuously reaffirm themselves and these principles and hold steady and consistent, true and faithful to their covenants, if they model true interdependence with each other as spouses, and truly love unconditionally but hang tough regarding the agreed-upon discipline system—if they do these things, in almost all cases the children will come around. They will know where the unconditional love supply is. They'll be grateful—even though they may not acknowledge it until they're on their missions or married—for the discipline and the limits that were established and the steadfastness of their parents.

Too many parents take rebellion and rejection personally, simply because they are too emotionally dependent themselves upon "belonging," upon acceptance by the children, and so a state of collusion is established wherein each parent feels validated by the weaknesses of the other; and they look about for friendly, sympathetic allies who agree with them and who massage their hearts and make them feel that they're okay and it's their "bratty kids" who aren't.

To be a producer requires independence. To be either a manager or a leader requires interdependence and a much higher level of maturity, but it presupposes that the person also possesses independence, so that he can think his own thoughts, derive his personal security from within, have a foundation of self-reliance and then willingly, happily, smilingly choose to communicate, to cooperate, to work with and through others, to be flexible, and to adapt to the human situation and the needs of others. Simply put, independent people can choose interdependency or not. Dependent people have no choice. They think they do but they're just "being lived." That is, they're living out programs or scripts handed to them.

Third Bermuda Triangle: No Leadership

The reason why this is Disasterville is that management alone is too logical, too cold, too left-brained, too amoral, too reliant upon systems, procedures, and checklists.

The real test of management and leadership is change. Changes upset and disturb people, stirring up fears, uncertainties, and insecurities. Changes need to be lubricated by leaders who know and care genuinely and who can empathize with the resisting concerns, who help others feel free to express their concerns and to get involved in problem analysis and the creation of new, acceptable solutions. Short of such leadership, the resistances will only solidify and crystallize and lead to a kind of fossilized, rigid bureaucracy in the family or a cold, logical, unsatisfying accommodation in the marriage.

There are simply too many well-managed families lacking leadership, proceeding correctly but in the wrong direction or full of excellent systems and checklists for everybody but with no heart, no warmth, no feeling. Children will tend to move away from these situations as soon as possible and may not desire to return, except maybe out of a sense of family duty or a strong spiritual desire to make some changes.

This phenomenon is also clearly evidenced in intergenerational family relationships, in which families naturally get together out of mutual interest and love and understanding, regularly see each other often, know each other, take an interest in each other's lives and concerns and hopes and disappointments. Or they get together only occasionally, somewhat begrudgingly out of a sense of duty or because of a common love for a grandparent or a special uncle or aunt who is still a magnet. In the latter case, as soon as that person is gone the spiritual umbrella is taken away and family members often simply go their separate ways, live in different cities, and feel closer to neighbors or old friends than they do to brothers or sisters or cousins or the remaining aunts and uncles.

The only thing that maintains influence over time is love in the innumerable ways it is expressed.

22

Four Family Systems: Goal Selection and Planning

Earlier we considered four divine models: Christ as a model for our personhood, our character; the Church as a model for our family organization; the temple as a model for our home; and the body, including all of nature, as a model for divine processes which we must go through in order to achieve the other three.

Let's examine the Church as a model organization on which to base our family organization. The Church is a magnificent institution. It is God's kingdom in the world. He gave it his Son's name and also the name of the Latter-day Saints, demonstrating the covenant relationship. It is our church as well as his, and if we are true and faithful to our covenants we will become co-inheritors with Christ of all that our Father has.

The Four Family Systems

The Church was set up by God, as is our family, and organized around divine principles. These principles have a practical, concrete manifestation in the form of goals or objectives, structure, and systems. I suggest if the four family systems as in the accompanying diagram are set up and properly *managed* and *led*, we will be following the essentials of the Church as a model organization.

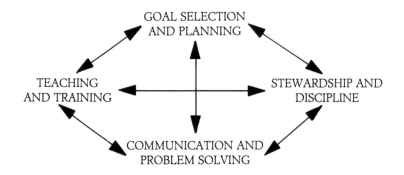

All four of the systems indicated are needed to make a family organization work. If one is left out or neglected, it will weaken the other three. The two-way arrows between all four systems connote their interdependent nature. To take away one of them would be analogous to eliminating one of the legs on a four-legged chair—the structure would topple.

For instance, if you did not have goals and plans, on what basis could you establish stewardships and a discipline program, or what would be the standards in teaching and training or in communicating and problem solving? If a family lacked a teaching and training program, how would you develop the skills of communication and problem solving or the willingness to take responsibilities or jobs, which we are calling stewardships, or to feel that the discipline system was fair and equitable? If you didn't have a system for communication and problem solving, when would you clarify values and select goals and make plans to achieve them? When would you do your teaching and training and set up various stewardships and carry out the agreed-upon disciplines? And finally, if you didn't have a system of stewardships and discipline, how would the work get done to accomplish goals and implement the plans, or to demonstrate and further develop the skills of communication and problem solving, or to have a practical arena or laboratory for teaching and training?

All four systems are absolutely necessary, but let's again think on Maslow's statement: "He that is good with a hammer tends to think everything is a nail." Many parents unwisely focus upon one or two of these systems, thinking that success in that system will compensate for failures in the other systems. People tend to do that which they are good at, that which they like doing, and to ask them to move outside their "comfort zone" can be very threatening and upsetting to them. But if someone will provide leadership and help lubricate the processes of growth and change, help them understand why they need all four systems, and encourage them to develop the new attitudes and skills which may lie outside their present scripts or their present modes of thinking and doing—if they get this help, their "new birth" processes will not be aborted because of the labor pains.

Interestingly, there are some activities which simultaneously involve and develop all four systems. In fact, these four systems are so interdependent that the moment you begin to work intensely in depth on any one of them, it will automatically involve the other three. For instance, good goal selection and planning will require a great deal of value clarification and priority setting. This, of course, will involve teaching, training, communication, and problem solving, and it will eventually result in different roles or stewardships needed to accomplish the goals and in agreed-upon consequences (discipline) when the roles are carried out or neglected.

Let's discuss each one of these systems in turn, recognizing continuously their interdependent nature. To fully understand each system requires an understanding of the other three systems, because the whole is more than the sum of its parts. It is the relationship between the systems which becomes a part in and of itself. The understanding and use of this insight is the essence of leadership as we have discussed it. Otherwise systems, however well managed, might fall apart because they lack the necessary glue of innovation and love which keeps them together.

Goal Selection and Planning

All things were created spiritually before they were created physically. This is why the goal selection and planning system is so basic and foundational. Isn't it an ironic thing that many individuals and almost all successful organizations have goals but most marriages and families do not? I'm not talking about abstract, ethereal, nebulous, general-principle-type goals, but rather about specific, clarified, well-defined and usually written, measurable, or discernible goals. Seriously think about it—have you and your spouse developed meaningful goals for your marriage, from which you can monitor yourselves, which you use continually for decision-making purposes, which give you a sense of direction and position and progress?

The Church is our model for a family organization, and it recently reaffirmed its basic three goals, They are written; they are measurable as well as discernible; they are specific and clear and give concrete reality to the Lord's transcendent goal of bringing to pass the immortality and eternal life of man.

These three broad goals are (1) to proclaim the gospel, (2) to perfect the Saints, and (3) to redeem the dead. You could well imagine how marriage and family goals could be, so to speak, the reciprocal of these three Church goals; that is, (1) to teach and live the gospel, (2) to assist each parent and child in perfecting their lives, and (3) to establish the intergenerational eternal family.

Regarding the Church's divine mission—to teach the gospel, perfect the Saints, and redeem the dead—the Church stresses four points of emphasis which give more specificity and concreteness: (1) spiritual welfare of the Saints, (2) temporal welfare of the Saints, (3) missionary work, and (4) genealogical research and temple work. Marriage could also develop four parallel points of emphasis, giving even more specificity to its goals. First, for the husband and the wife: to continually develop and deepen their spirituality as individuals and as eternal companions. Second, to adequately take care of the present and future temporal welfare of each family member. Third, to prepare themselves and their children to continuously teach the gospel, whether it be in their own home through the family home evening program, the homes of their member neighbors through home teaching, or with nonmember neighbors through missionary work. Fourth, in preparing genealogies, books of remembrance, family and personal histories; in participating in the name extraction program as requested; and in regularly doing temple ordinances as far back as possible for their own family as well as for others in the family of Adam.

The marvelous thing about goals is how they clarify where we're going and where we now are. They are a form of spiritual creation. In building a house we must first have the blueprint, then every day we go to the construction shed to study it to get our marching orders for that day. Similarly, goals serve as a blueprint. We begin each day with the end in mind. Many people give lip service to goal selection but do little about it simply because doing it right takes tremendous discipline, a spirit of cooperation, of interdependency, of maturity, and of communication.

Regarding family goals, I suggest the underlying principle is, "Without involvement there is no commitment." Unless people feel that they have had some say in the formation of goals that will govern them, guide them, lead them, measure their progress, they will not be committed. You cannot normally give other people their goals. If they identify with you to an extremely high extent, then you might give them their goals. But to achieve that level of identification requires a high degree of involvement, the building of an emotional bank account over time, so in the last analysis the fundamental principle is the same: Without involvement there is no commitment.

We teach people correct principles; we should allow them to select and be governed by goals congruent with those principles. Then they will be committed, internally motivated. When children are very young their identification with their parents is extremely high. Parents can pretty well hand them scripts in the form of goal-role statements. But as they grow up, many variables come into play, and the less authoritarian the parents are, the more they can utilize the perspectives and processes of the gospel. These are not democratic processes as the world understands democracy; and they certainly aren't permissive or laissez-faire practices as the world understands those terms. But neither are they authoritarian practices. They basically involve the other three systems spoken about: teaching and training; communication and problem solving; and the establishment of stewardships and the accountability processes which bring discipline (discipleship) to the family setting.

The worldly continuum of leadership goes from authoritarian through democratic to laissez-faire. This is a false secular motion. By examining our four divine models, we discover a much higher long-term process of divine influence. It is God-centered, priesthood-directed, love-motivated. It is based on building emotional bank accounts and striving for consensus. It is based on teaching correct principles and letting others govern themselves. It is based on teaching through modeling and relating, primarily; telling, secondarily. It is based on the principle of mutual consent.

If you want to look at a magnificent illustration of the divine model, look at how people are brought into the Church. Is the process democratic? No. Is it authoritarian? No. Is it laissez-faire? No. That whole continuum of thinking is obsolete. People are brought into the Church when they are taught with love and testimony and the Spirit works upon them as they strive to keep their commitments. The whole process lubricates the steps of change within them so that they come to understand, to be edified, and to know of the truth and vitality of the gospel in their life. Then they willingly choose to covenant. They do that in the waters of baptism, and the Lord confirms it in the confirmation blessing by giving his Holy Spirit to them as a guide and companion as long as they seek it and live true to it.

This magnificent conversion model is the key to family life and to marriage. We should always treat our children as if they were investigators and follow the same principles that missionaries use in working with investigators. You can't force investigators; you can't ridicule and embarrass and punish them for their stupidity, their laziness, their slothfulness. You may, however, be inspired to reprove them "with sharpness when moved upon by the Holy Ghost," but you will immediately desire to reaffirm your love so that they will know there is nothing personal about it; you simply are hanging tough on divine standards and principles, and everything is geared to their happiness, growth, and development. As with missionaries and investigators, so in the home—there is nothing arbitrary or artificial; nothing is done to satisfy the ego of a parent for control and dominion—everything is based upon divine law. The ultimate end is the child's happiness and optimal growth.

Another excellent illustration of the divine model comes to us when we watch the operations of the Church itself. Watch how a stake is reorganized. It is an absolutely amazing process—nothing less than a miracle—that within a twenty-four-hour period a stake can change its leadership and end up on a higher plane. It simply does not normally take place in human organizations. There it may take months, even years, to change the leadership at the top. There is often a great deal of politicking and influence-peddling, lobbying, speculating. In a stake reorganization some members' minds may be focused on these things, but the divine process itself is not. It is magnificent and truly divine. While the process is conducted under authority, it is not an authoritarian process. The General Authorities present preside, but they work with the above-mentioned principles continually, and the Spirit lubricates the processes in the hearts and minds of the faithful. And an increase of unity and commitment usually results. I have personally witnessed several of these experiences on a firsthand basis and can bear testimony of the divine magnificence of the process.

For another scripture model, study how a Church call is given and received. Again we see celestial principles of love, understanding, and commitment being carried out. This is the essence of how the father should preside or give assignments or calls. The secular authoritarian, democratic, laissez-faire continuum is a telestial continuum designed for the telestial world in which we live. I believe there are many organizations which rise to a terrestrial level and which use some of the processes and principles we have discussed. I think the best organizations today strive for mutual consent or consensus on vital issues. The principle of participation and involvement is deeply established in the psyche of most progressive managers and leaders in industry today. Part of it is an effort to deal with strong competition from Japan, where companies have been using these principles for years, many of which they learned and adapted from America.

But a marriage and a family which has been set up under God's law can go even further, can go into a celestial level of operation. It will operate very much as a good ward or stake operates, or as the Brethren operate when they set the Church in order —authoritative but not authoritarian. This is the spirit of marriage and family management and leadership. And basic to family governance is spiritual creation.

Put simply, the first system is to involve the family in developing a clear conception of what we are about in our marriage and in our family.

23

Four Family Systems: Teaching and Training

The second of the four systems described in chapter 22 is that of teaching and training. Just as the Lord is our divine model for teaching and training, so parents must carry this responsibility for their children. This is the divine pattern. This is the way it should be and this is the way it will be, for good or for ill, for parents give their scripts to their children. If the parents do not get their scripts from the Lord's scripts as contained in the true scripts, or scriptures, great distortions will take place; and unhappiness, confusion, and transgression will emerge, perhaps to the third or fourth generation.

There is a difference between teaching and training. Teaching deals with the what and the why; training, with the how. Teaching deals with correct principles; training, with skills, with how-to's. Teaching deals with knowledge and attitudes; training deals more with skills.

Three Kinds of Problems

One of the most important distinctions parents need to learn is the three kinds of problems they may have with their children.

The first one we could call a value problem; it attempts to answer the question, "*Should* the child do it?" The second one we could call a competence problem having to do with the question, "*Can* the child do it?" The third becomes a motivational problem having to do with the question, "Does the child *want* to do it?"

It is important not to confuse one of these questions with the other. One child might know that he should take care of the yard, and even know how to do it, but not want to do it. Another child may know how to mow the lawn but doesn't feel he should mow the lawn (perhaps because he did it last week or he doesn't think it needs it) and therefore doesn't want to do it. Another child may want to repair the sprinkler, knows it should be repaired, but simply doesn't know how to do it.

The first key in solving any problem is to diagnose it correctly. You wouldn't bring in a cardiologist if you had a foot problem. You wouldn't bring in an ophthalmologist if you had a back problem. You wouldn't bring in a plumber if the roof leaked, or an electrician if your car was out of gas. Neither would you attempt to solve a skill or competency problem with a value solution; or a motivational problem with a skill or training solution; or a value problem with a motivational solution.

But remember yet again Maslow's wise statement: "He who is good with a hammer tends to think everything is a nail." Many people have a solution and they're looking for a problem that fits it. Though they may have a good solution, they're working on the wrong problem. But they're deeply scripted. They feel comfortable in applying that solution and very uncomfortable in diagnosing the nature of the problem.

One time I found myself criticizing my very young son for throwing all of his clothes in a heap in the center of the floor of his room. I continued to give the value solution: "Don't you realize, son, you shouldn't do this? Do you realize what will happen when your clothes get wrinkled and dirty like this?" You should, you should, you should! He didn't resist me; he didn't rebel—he agreed. Still, day in and day out, his clothes were in a heap. I even sensed he wanted to do as I asked, but I never really questioned whether he could, whether it was a problem of competency.

One day I thought to myself, "Maybe he simply does not know how to hang up his clothes. He's just a little kid." So I took about a half an hour to train him at how to hang up his clothes. He enjoyed the training. We even took the clothes down again and then hung them back up again. He now knew how to take the pants of his little Sunday suit by the cuffs and hang them over the lower wire of the clothes hanger and put the hanger on the lower bar of the closet. I taught him how to take his shirt and button it up the front, turn it over, fold one-third of each side of the shirt towards the center, and fold the sleeves in, then lay the shirt in his drawer. He enjoyed the process, as we had a good feeling with each other and he was learning and I wasn't belittling or moralizing or preaching or condemning. It represented a substantial deposit in the emotional bank account. It also stirred up the motivation or the desire to do on his own what he had learned.

Years later this same son had the same problem again, but the nature of it was no longer competency; it was motivational, and it took a motivational solution to solve it. I suggest that in most instances a value-type problem ("Should I do it?") is solved in the quality of the relationship, or what we have been calling the emotional bank account. The solution is a teaching solution, but 95 percent of teaching is modeling and relating, or building the emotional bank account, and perhaps only 5 or 10 percent is telling. In other words, scripting is the key to most value problems, because goals are formed on values, which is another word for "should I?"

I suggest that almost all competency problems are amenable to training. However, a training solution usually requires a positive emotional bank account as well, which to some degree is built on the teaching relationship. "Whom can I teach but my friends?"

The motivational problem of "Do I want to?" is a function of managing consequences. The underlying principle is that behavior is a function of its consequences, temporal or spiritual. If in working to "make a living" we found no "living" forthcoming, we simply wouldn't continue doing that particular work. How much of the temple work of the world would get done if people weren't spiritually repaid? If our children don't want to do their jobs, in all likelihood it's because there are few, if any, meaningful positive consequences for doing them, or few, if any, consistently applied negative consequences for not doing them. Or perhaps the trade-off consequences for not doing the job are more acceptable than are those for doing them. (We will discuss basic consequences in much greater depth when we go into the stewardship and discipline systems.)

Teaching Children to Pray

Before concluding this material on teaching and training, let's illustrate these transferable processes and principles by some ideas about a preeminently important stewardship of parents—that of teaching children to pray. Here I must of necessity introduce experiences from my own family, but I do this merely to illustrate the points and certainly with no sense of suggesting that ours is the perfect pattern or that we have achieved great success with it. In fact the whole thing is still a daily struggle.

To my mind, no other single activity has such a determining influence on the whole of life as does effective prayer. It can and should determine everything else, including our actions and our attitudes or responses to all that happens to us. If it is neglected, everything else in life is negatively affected. If it is honored, everything else in life is graced. It is no wonder God commands parents to "teach their children to pray, and to walk uprightly before the Lord" (D&C 68:28).

I believe that many of us in the Church are having problems and unhappiness because we are not properly teaching our children, and before we will be released from these plaguing problems we will need to "set in order" our own homes. Most of us know in our hearts that this is true, even though we consciously focus on "outside" problems—work, finances, Church assignments, and so on. Carefully study the eleven verses of counsel the Lord gave to the First Presidency (Joseph Smith, Sidney Rigdon, and Frederick G. Williams) and Bishop Newel K. Whitney along these lines:

But I have commanded you to bring up your children in light and truth.

But verily I say unto you, my servant Frederick G. Williams, you have continued under this condemnation;

You have not taught your children light and truth, according to the commandments; and that wicked one hath power, as yet, over you, and this is the cause of your affliction.

And now a commandment I give unto you—if you will be delivered you shall set in order your own house, for there are many things that are not right in your house.

Verily, I say unto my servant Sidney Rigdon, that in some things he hath not kept the commandments concerning his children; therefore, first set in order thy house.

Verily, I say unto my servant Joseph Smith, Jun., or in other words, I will call you friends, for you are my friends, and ye shall have an inheritance with me—

I called you servants for the world's sake, and ye are their servants for my sake—

And now, verily I say unto Joseph Smith, Jun.—You have not kept the commandments, and must needs stand rebuked before the Lord;

Your family must needs repent and forsake some things, and give more earnest heed unto your sayings, or be removed out of their place.

What I say unto one I say unto all; pray always lest that wicked one have power in you, and remove you out of your place.

My servant Newel K. Whitney also, a bishop of my church, hath need to be chastened, and set in order his family, and see that they are more diligent and concerned at home, and pray always, or they shall be removed out of their place. (D&C 93:40-50.)

In these eleven verses the Lord declares, "What I say unto one I say unto all."

My wife tells the following story:

❢ On one occasion Stephen was going out of town for a short business trip. It was late Friday afternoon and he was delayed at his office longer than had been expected. He dashed home and we frantically got him packed and organized.

He hadn't time to see or visit with any of the children, and now, with the pressure of that plane leaving with or without him, he called for family prayer.

It was not the usual time for prayer, and the children were scattered all over the house and outside. I ran to the door and tried to get the boys in from playing football on the front lawn. Someone else was in the middle of a TV show and hated to leave it. One was on the telephone, resenting the interruption; another was jumping on the trampoline with friends; and someone else was taking a nap.

Stephen was totally frustrated. He shouted at the boys on the lawn. "For heaven's sake, will you get in here—right now! When I call for family prayer that means to drop what you're doing and come. I've got a plane to catch."

Then I started in. "What's the matter with you kids, anyway?" Our voices were rising higher and louder with each phrase.

By the time we were all kneeling together there was a dark cloud of gloom, bad feelings, guilt, and frustration hanging over us all. Nobody felt like praying. "Maria, will you pray?" A pause. "I really don't feel like it—could you call on someone else?"

Stephen glanced around at the wounded faces and realized what had happened. He began to apologize. "I'm sorry I yelled. It's just that I don't want to leave without seeing all of you, having a prayer, asking for a blessing of safety in traveling, and feeling everything is in order."

As he went on, we all started searching our hearts. He had such a good, sincere motive. Why couldn't we have been more cooperative and less selfish? Gradually all hearts were softened.

The prayer was short. All he asked for was forgiveness. He left immediately.

We all felt bad when he left. We all wanted a better ending to the situation, and now we really wished we could have knelt together and prayed fully and openly with a good spirit. Our hearts ached. It was too late. But we had learned something.

Teaching is not telling, of course. Certainly it is not yelling. The fundamental principle of teaching our children to pray is to be truly praying people ourselves. We teach what we are. Are our prayers earnest, deep, meaningful, and two-way? Are our lives anchored and committed by them? Are we changed through them? We teach what we are.

My wife and I have concluded that it is supremely important to have both personal and husband-wife prayers before greeting the children in the morning. In those prayers we seek to get our own spirits in tune with the Lord's Spirit so that we are at peace within ourselves and between ourselves. Once we feel the Spirit, we then attempt to walk through our day in our mind's eye. We determine our attitudes and responses to unpleasant situations or to a difficult child. To use computer language, we try to "program ourselves" with true principles and commitments while under the divine influence of the Holy Spirit.

For instance, if you have the tendency to yell at your children when they disobey, or at your spouse when he or she doesn't meet your expectations, even though you rationalize your actions while "in the heat of the battle," you know within that such a belittling approach is foolish, futile, and self-perpetuating (the more you do it, the more you'll have to do it). Yet you still do it. It becomes a habit, and others develop habitual ways of defending themselves against it. Children become threat deaf. They (and spouses) yell back, walk out, or "get back" in some other way.

Through deep, meaningful prayer we can "spiritually create" a far more effective response. We can "see" ourselves reacting on the basis of the Savior's nature and principles. Through such an approach, "line upon line, precept upon precept," we can become "partakers of the divine nature" (2 Peter 1:4). "When a man works by faith he works by mental exertion instead of physical force. It is by words, instead of exerting his physical powers, with which every being works when he works by faith." (*Lectures on Faith*, 7:3.)

There is no doubt that such gospel living will have ten times more impact in teaching children to pray than any number of practical techniques.

In mortality, children's first source of knowledge of God is human—their parents. The second source is divine—revelation from God. (Study the Second Lecture on Faith.) I have observed from missionaries, students, and investigators that if the first source is distorted (unkind, hypocritical), so also will be the concept of God in the minds of the children as they mature. They will then pray with this wrong conception of God. If they are fearful to be open and honest with their parents because of receiving over-reactive, angry responses, they will learn not to be open and honest in prayer to God. Their divine communications will likely be as mechanical and protective and manipulative as their human communications.

I am persuaded that children's divine conceptions are largely a product of how their parents treat them, particularly under con-ditions of stress. Teaching by example and unconditional love, reinforced by precept, is again the key.

Children are constantly investigating our lives to see if the gospel is true. "I don't care how much you know about prayer until I know how much you care about me."

Just as there are different levels of human communication, there are different levels of divine communication. Perhaps it's more a matter of degree, but for purposes of analysis I arbitrarily select the following three levels:

1. Mechanical prayer
2. Meaningful one-way heartfelt expression
3. Genuine two-way communication

As parents, we need regular experiences at the third level in order to understand and appreciate the orderly sequential growth through these levels and also to develop the sensitivity and skill with our children to facilitate these growth processes. Consider each one.

1. *Mechanical prayer.* We teach our children to "say" their prayers. So they learn to "say" their prayers. They are acquiring a helpful discipline. They "say" their prayers when they get up and when they go to bed, perhaps at their parent's knee or side. They should see their parents call everyone for family prayer and perhaps sense a higher level of prayer. They should see and hear a blessing offered on the food at each meal. In such a home God is recognized, acknowledged. They sense this. This is good. It is a good beginning. They are acquiring the most basic habit and discipline of spiritual life. We need to teach our children what missionaries teach investigators—the four steps of prayer:

a. "Our Father in Heaven . . . "
b. "We thank thee . . . "
c. "We ask thee . . . "
d. "In the name of Jesus Christ. Amen."

2. *Meaningful one-way heartfelt expression.* If as parents we are kind and patient, open and grateful, we can teach a much higher level of prayer to our children. We essentially are teaching them to pray from their hearts rather than to say the same words again and again, like going down some kind of checklist. My wife and I have found some of the following ideas or types of expressions helpful in teaching our children how to pray from the heart. Remember, these practices we have found helpful in our family, but other family situations may respond better to different practices.

When we call for prayers, we are interrupting the lives of many people involved in various tasks and projects. Everyone has his mind focused on what he was doing, and we need to take a few minutes to prepare ourselves for prayer. A parent may say to his children, "Let's take a few moments to think about whom we are praying to and why. Let's quietly think about what we are doing —about the things we are grateful for." We need to pause, to become calm and still inside. Otherwise we bring the rush of life into our prayers, keeping us at the mechanical level.

In our home, usually we sing a hymn before family prayer, such as "Sweet Hour of Prayer" or "I Need Thee Every Hour" or "Love at Home." This gives the children time to gather around mentally as well as physically. It helps to bring some unity and harmony and order to the entire situation. The family seems to enjoy this, although we sometimes omit it if time pressures are too heavy.

Often we go around the prayer circle and ask each family member if he has any special needs or blessings he would like to have remembered in the prayer. This process helps us to be aware of everyone's needs and to pray specifically.

We often guide a little child before the prayer. "Think about what is in your heart and say it to your Heavenly Father." Or,

"David, what are you really grateful for? How has the Lord blessed our family and answered our prayers? Let's think about it, and then just talk to your Heavenly Father as you talk to me. Don't worry if you don't say everything everyone else says. Say what you really feel in your heart. Heavenly Father loves and cares for you just as I do—even more so."

In appropriate ways we commend the children for spontaneous, heartfelt expression. Yet we try to be careful not to cause them to gear their expressions to our ears and for our reward. "Your Father in Heaven is pleased when you tell him how you really feel." "That was nice, honey. Your Heavenly Father loves to hear you pray to him in that way." When we do this, we sense that the children feel doubly appreciated.

Sometimes we have found our children offering essentially the same mechanical prayer in every situation. We believe this is due in part to our own "vain repetitions" and also in part to their becoming tired and/or bored in listening too long to general prayers, however sincerely expressed.

When we notice mechanical prayers, we make a serious effort to break them up. They can become so habitual and reinforcing as to work into people's consciences and make them feel guilty and uncomfortable if they are not "on their knees" or "in the right spirit" or "in the right place" or if they don't remember the entire checklist—loved ones, missionaries, leaders, and so on.

We should all try to teach by example and precept that we can pray anywhere, anytime—and that we should. "Pray always" means a constant, subconscious commitment to and awareness of the Lord, so that his purposes and principles govern our every action, word, and thought, plus a frequent conscious renewal of that relationship and commitment in prayer.

We generally find that prayer is a golden teaching moment. On a one-to-one basis the children are very open to comments such as: "Son, you can pray while you're walking." "You can pray with your eyes open." "You can pray out loud or silently within." "You can pray for help to get out of a bad mood." "Son, learn to go alone at least once a day (preferably more often) where no one else can see you or hear you except your Father in Heaven. I do this, son. Sometimes I go. . . . ''

After family prayer it may be appropriate to remain kneeling for personal prayers, as is common among missionaries. Or you might say to your children, ''Suppose each of us goes to a very private place for personal private prayer for a few minutes.'' The Savior taught his ''children'' (disciples) to do this (see Matthew 6:5-8).

We find praying alone, out loud, sometimes helps to discipline and focus our minds, but that it doesn't seem necessary once we're in the Spirit. Words then seem to limit deeper-feeling expression.

We have often tried to teach our children to pray in terms of their needs rather than their wants: ''What is best for my character, my development, my spiritual growth, even if it's a hard experience for me?'' The Lord knows what we need—we know what we want. This is one excellent reason for regular scripture study. The Lord is constantly dealing with his children in terms of their needs, not their wants.

This is pretty hard doctrine for any of us, and it was especially hard for one of our teenage daughters. Being elected cheerleader of her high school seemed to be the most important need in her life. She had worked for several months, practicing every day doing cartwheels, flips, splits, and cheers until we were all relieved when the final cuts came. There were tears every time one of her close friends was eliminated, and hope surged as she progressed to the final election assembly. ''Oh mother, I'm praying so hard to win. The Lord says you can ask for any righteous desire of your heart, and this is mine.'' It seemed a reasonable request to us, too. She was firm and solid in the Church and socially popular in a sophisticated and large high school. We thought she would be a good influence for the Church.

At the final assembly tryouts, things went beautifully. She was in great form, her cheer was original, she was well known, and she received as much applause as or more than anyone else. She seemed a cinch to be one of the five winners.

She was absolutely crushed when she lost. It was only by a few votes, but she lost.

"Mother, you just don't know how important this was to me," she sobbed. "It's one of my lifetime goals. Why did the Lord let me down when I prayed so fervently? It wasn't just for myself. I was going to use this office as a good, solid influence for the Church. I study the scriptures every single night. I do missionary work constantly. I stand up for the Church in every situation. I work my head off in the ward and the seminary council. And then one time when I ask for help, what do I get? It isn't as if I didn't do my part. I practiced for six months. I couldn't have tried harder."

My wife remembers, "I was a little disillusioned myself. So good. So faithful. So deserving. I didn't have too many answers, but I told her there must be a good reason, and through prayer and study she would come to understand why."

The next month she was asked to be one of the high school seminary officers. All of the seminary council had made personal sacrifices to serve. The seminary president had been asked to give up running for studentbody president; this was a hard decision for him. They said they really needed our daughter's creativity and missionary talents to draw people, and this year was a crucial one for gaining a positive stronghold.

That year she had many profound spiritual experiences. She developed deep, meaningful friendships and was a positive influence in helping several people come into Church activity.

Later she told me that she gradually came to an understanding of herself through fervent prayer and study of the scriptures. "I wanted to be a cheerleader more than anything else, but perhaps the Lord knew I needed this other experience more. I needed more spiritual growth. It was a hard experience, but I feel in my heart it was right."

3. *Genuine two-way communication.* In two-way prayer we listen and respond to what we hear. Perhaps in many of our one-way prayers we counsel the Lord, directing him around the heavens and the earth, telling him whom to bless and how.

There seem to be two basic principles in teaching children this level of prayer: first, having them experience the satisfaction of two-way communication with their parents; second, helping them understand how to listen to the voice of the Lord and how to recognize it.

A person's satisfaction with something is primarily a function of his expectation, over which he has control, and secondarily a product of his realization, over which he may not have control.

We need to create accurate expectations in our children's minds regarding how the Lord speaks to us, so that they will recognize his voice and feel satisfied when they hear (sense, feel) it. Prayer will then become deeply meaningful and satisfying. Otherwise, if they expect something more dramatic and physical, something mysterious and strange, and don't realize their expectations, they will pray only out of duty and not out of desire. Their prayers will become mechanical monologues. Talking to oneself, to the ceiling, or to the mattress is boring and unfulfilling.

We need to teach our children that the Lord speaks to us in many ways but more particularly through his servants, the prophets—ancient (scriptures) and modern (conferences, writings)—and through his still, small voice. We need to teach them that their heart is the ear of the Spirit and that their divine conscience is his voice.

My wife and I are trying to teach our children to test their actions and attitudes and plans against their consciences to see if they square up. We are trying to teach them to ask basic questions and listen to their consciences for the answer to questions such as, "What do I need to do to be closer to God?" "How can I be a better member of the Church?" "How can I better prepare for my mission?" "How can I do better in school?"

We encourage our children to first seek the Holy Spirit by asking for it and then allowing it to guide their expressions and listening.

We are trying to teach them to continually educate their consciences through paying close attention at Church meetings and by studying the scriptures—really feasting on the words and the love of Jesus Christ. In this way their consciences will become repositories of divine principle that the Holy Ghost will bring to their remembrance to guide and direct their paths. We are encouraging them to memorize many key passages that are filled with wisdom pertaining to their present opportunities and challenges. We review these in family home evening.

We are trying to teach them that we do not receive more light and knowledge until we are true to the light and knowledge we already have. In other words, let's just obey our consciences, and if we need more the Lord will give it to us in his way and in his time, not in our way and time.

Finally, we are encouraging them to respond to what they "hear" in their prayers by committing themselves to obey the divine principle or directive given and then to "report back" on that commitment in a later prayer.

We find that such a relationship based on communication requires infinitely more courage and humility, determination, and self-honesty than one-way prayers from the heart. Such true living and communication is also infinitely more satisfying, sanctifying, and empowering.

Once a person discovers the possibility of a dynamic, living relationship and communication, once he learns the special meaning of mighty prayer, he is never the same again. All things, including relationships, are changed and made infinitely more alive and beautiful.

My wife and I have learned and are learning much in the process of teaching our children to pray. Most importantly, we have learned (or had the knowledge confirmed) that we are about as successful in our efforts to teach our children the genuine dialogue level as we in *our* praying and living at this level. That perhaps is the most appropriate note on which to end this chapter on teaching and training through God-centered leadership. For Church leaders of all kinds and for all who seek to influence others toward a better way, there is still no substitute for example.

24

Four Family Systems: Communication and Problem-Solving Systems

Communication is the single most important activity in life. It undergirds every other activity. And our success as communicators will pretty well determine our success in life—particularly in marriage and family life. We might well imagine some technical jobs which do not require great communication skills. But we can't imagine great marriage and family life without communication at its heart. Let's focus particularly on two vital communication activities. First, the one-on-one visits, and second, the family meetings such as family councils and family home nights.

One on One

The one on one is the real key. The moment you introduce even one other person into this special relationship it changes its essential character and nature. Then both people begin to adapt themselves to the presence of the third or more. Consider the nature of private prayer: it's one on one. Consider marriage itself: it's one with one. Consider the value of a private date with each child, a private lunch, a private special activity wherein total attention is focused upon that child, upon that child's interests, concerns, needs, hopes, fears, and doubts.

There is a compelling mountain scene poster with the invitation at the bottom: "Let the mountain have you for a day." Magnificent nature draws us into itself. We feel more relaxed, more at peace, more tranquil, more at home. The same thing takes place in a human relationship with one other person. Let's change the slogan to: "Let your child have you for an hour," "Let your teenager have you for an evening." In this mode, in a relaxed state of mind you are in a sense letting the other have his or her way with you. I'm not talking about compromising principles or becoming soft and permissive and indulging a child's whims and interests. Obviously, such a thing would be wrong. What I am talking about is to be completely present with the other person, and to transcend your own personal interests and concerns and fears and needs and ego. Be fully with your wife, son, or daughter, allowing them to have their interests and goals expressed or worked on, subordinating your own to that end.

If I were to attempt to summarize the key influence activity of them all, it would simply be the "one on one." This would pertain to a relationship with God, with one's spouse, with a friend, or with a child. If you neglect the one on ones and do excellently in group settings, I suggest few significant deposits will be made into the emotional bank accounts. Relationships may even deteriorate. But if you do excellently in the one on ones, you could botch up many of the other situations and still come out shining. Of course, the desirable state is to strive for excellence in both the one on ones and the group settings. But most important, perhaps ten times as important as the group setting, is the one on one.

Think about it with regard to prayer. The Lord said that the most deep, meaningful prayers we can express are offered in our closet between us and God alone. Notice what happens when other people are present in our prayers. Do we not become somewhat focused upon their presence, their thinking, their minds? Oftentimes we may find ourselves almost praying to them—more conscious of their presence and what they think of our prayers than in praying deeply from our heart to our Heavenly Father. When we pray all alone, our real intent, our sincerity, our fundamental identity, is best manifest. Likewise when you are one on one with your spouse or your child and are fully attending to that person's needs and interests and goals, then allowing him or her to attend to your needs and interests and goals, it becomes a mutually serving and a mutually edifying experience. In this way we are tapping into the divine model or principle of prayer, private worship, and communion. And we are dealing with the fundamental roots of influence.

For many years now my wife and I have had a little one-on-one practice which we thoroughly enjoy and look forward to with anticipation, eagerness, and excitement. We do it as frequently as we can. We get out our little trail cycle, which we can both get on. It is almost noiseless, so we can talk easily to each other without any straining whatsoever, and we simply putt-putt around the neighborhood and visit. This is the way we "get away" for some one-on-one talking; other couples naturally will choose the way that suits them best.

On these visits my wife and I talk about everything, whether it be just temporary issues of the day or long-range concerns or self-doubts or fears. We often share differing perceptions of the same situation as we role-play more effective approaches to difficult interpersonal family problems. For instance, I may act as if I am a son or daughter requesting a special privilege even though I haven't fulfilled a basic family responsibility, and my wife will play herself. We thus interact back and forth so as to train ourselves in being consistent in modeling and teaching correct principles. Our best role plays come from redoing a past difficult or stressful scene in which we might have "blown it." In our talks too we get any negative or buried feelings out in the open so that we can talk about them and come to understand how each of us feels about it and sees it.

We've developed a useful practice to handle the situation when we find a large difference in our priorities on a non-critical matter. We ask each other how we would rank the strength of our feeling on a ten-point scale regarding that particular issue or point. For instance, if my wife is terribly excited about going to a ballet and I would prefer staying home, we will ask each other, "On a ten-point scale, how strong is your feeling?" We have agreed up front on two things: that we will be totally honest and that we will defer to the one with the stronger feeling, assuming that discussion doesn't change the ranking. So if she says eight and I say three, we go to the ballet. If I say seven and she says five, we stay home. In other words, we are giving a great deal of weight to how deeply we each feel about a particular matter.

Remember, the democratic one-man-one-vote approach is not God's way of governing a family. His approach is through kindness and gentleness and two-way communication, and gaining mutual understanding, and trying to think of solutions that benefit both parties. His approach is for us to have respect for the strength of the feeling of one another and to be willing to subordinate one's own feeling. His approach is called selflessness and consideration and gentleness. It is not voting, nor is it exercising unrighteous dominion in the name of priesthood, nor is it asserting rights, whether real or imagined.

Later in this book we will go deeper into the communication skill and the importance of listening with empathy. Suffice it to say at this point, however, that the tendency for most people in one on ones is to seek first to be understood. If I were to summarize in one sentence the single most important learning of my own work in this particular field in the last quarter of a century it would be put in this way: seek first to understand, then to be understood.

I like to remember the prayer of St. Francis of Assisi, who said, "Help me, oh God, to realize that it is in understanding another that I will be understood." Most people do the very opposite. They seek first to be understood. And when both parties are seeking to be understood simultaneously, we have what we might call a collective monologue—or what the French call "the dialogue of the deaf."

It is risky business to listen fully to another person, because it makes us soft and tender. It exposes our vulnerabilities. We may be changed. And if down deep we are feeling fairly insecure, we can't afford the risk of being changed. We need the sense of pre- dictability and certainty. That is the anatomy of prejudice or pre- judgment. We must judge beforehand so that we don't have to deal with the possibility of a new thing happening. The specter of change frightens most people.

However, the more we are inwardly secure and invulnerable down deep, the more we can afford the risks of being vulnerable on the surface of our life. When we have the armor of God deep inside our nature, we are not too worried about protecting our ego. The key to listening is to listen with the intent to under- stand, not with the intent to reply. We will discuss this in greater depth later on. But it is the very essence of a successful one on one, particularly if you are dealing with problems and with dif- ferences.

Family Meetings

The second most important meeting is the family meeting, which I divide into two kinds. First, the family council, where we attempt to make decisions by consensus as much as possible and to try to hammer out solutions which satisfy all those concerned; where we model how to give and take, how to listen to each other, how to generate new solutions which have mutual benefit in them; where we do scheduling, planning, value clarifying and goal selection, resolving of differences, setting family rules or policies or procedures and determining fair consequences and the correct discipline system; where jobs or stewardships are estab- lished and reported on in a consistent accountability process.

The family home evening serves a different function, even though the two meetings conceivably could be brought together for simplification purposes. In our family we find it is better to involve the children in the family council after they reach the age of about twelve. It makes them feel special, as if they are carrying a unique responsibility, as do the parents for the little children. and with these additional responsibilities come special privileges and rights. Sometimes we have to be flexible on this matter, however, finding that a particular issue at hand should involve younger children in the discussion.

The family home evening is more for the purpose of teaching values and gospel principles, displaying talents, and enjoying different kinds of family fun and activities. It is not primarily a time for decision making and problem solving. We have also learned, sometimes the hard way, that neither of these meetings should be held at dinner time. As far as possible, dinner time should be upbeat and positive and not a place for moralizing, correcting, or even verbal teaching. It is a place for pleasant interaction and conversation and sharing.

The problem with many families, however, is that dinner time is about the only time they ever get together for anything. So they attempt to combine into that one setting the one on one, the family council, and the family home evening. They are attempting to serve all purposes with one basic tool. They will find they will serve none of these purposes very well and won't enjoy their food much either.

The Church has an outstanding resource book for family home evenings. If these are carefully planned and the children are involved in participating in significant ways in the different phases of a family home evening; and if everyone puts a priority on the time, and if the time is respected when they are to be held, when they are to begin, and basically when they are to end (with some flexibility); and if generally there is a positive, upbeat spirit present and the parents don't use the meetings to berate and lecture their children; and if there are refreshments and an activity that gives some fun; and if the program doesn't take a disproportionate amount of time so that it infringes too much on other important activities or on private time—if these criteria are satisfied, our experience is that family home evenings are very positive and are basic in helping to create a beautiful, celestial family spirit and culture.

25

Four Family Systems: The Stewardship/Discipline System

The word *stewardship* is a spiritual and a sacred word. It evolves out of a theological concept or principle. A steward is one who has a special trust, a special responsibility, and an accountability on that responsibility. When we consecrate all that we have to the Lord for the building of his kingdom, then we no longer really possess anything, including ourselves and our time, talents, and possessions. He then gives us everything back in the form of a stewardship and asks us, from time to time, to give an accounting on that stewardship, whether it be our taking care of our own body (which really he paid for with a terrible price), or our income, which he asks only a tithe on, or our relationships, as in our marriages and families.

The word *discipline* has roots similar to that of the word *disciple*, which has a theological foundation. To the Latter-day Saint, the purpose of discipline is not to punish or get back at someone for what he has done to us. The purpose of discipline is to produce a disciple of the Lord—one who is trained and nurtured in His ways.

It is very important to understand the spiritual nature of these two words before we attempt to discuss the stewardship/discipline system, so that we have the correct perspective and the right feeling. If we attempt to set up a stewardship/discipline system at home without this perspective and feeling, we will violate the essence of it and almost have to resort to a system of jobs, rewards and punishments, and nagging, which over time can be a constant headache, a source of harassment, irritation, and a great deal of negative energy.

Therefore, with this perspective in mind, whenever we speak here about a particular chore or job a person has, we really mean a stewardship. When we talk about follow-up or follow-through, we mean accountability. When we talk about discipline, we mean the consistent application of agreed-upon consequences, which can serve in a sense as the Law of Moses did, as a schoolmaster to bring people to Christ or to true discipleship. The tone is positive and upbeat.

Win/Win

Before we present the specifics surrounding the stewardship/discipline system, we need to discuss one other principle which pertains equally to the communication/problem-solving system: the principle of win/win. Win/win basically means that we go for agreements or solutions which are mutually beneficial—that both parties feel good about. The traditional approach is win/lose, which means: I win, you lose; I feel good about it, you don't; but I'm the boss and can't think too much about what you think or feel; you should do it just because I'm the boss and I told you to. That is a win/lose system.

A win/lose stewardship or job would be a situation in which I think you should do it, I feel good about it, but you don't. You don't think you *should* do it, or you don't think you *can* do it, and you certainly don't *want* to do it. That is a win/lose job.

The opposite of win/lose is lose/win. It means permissiveness and capitulation. Giving up, giving in. It means being "a nice guy." The expression goes that "nice guys finish last." This is often the case because they think lose/win. They like to please or appease other people. They have little courage or strength of their own to express their own feelings and convictions. They are intimidated by the ego strength of others or by how adamant others may be in expressing their feelings and convictions. So they tend to give in. This is lose/win.

The problem is that unexpressed feelings don't die. They are buried alive and come forth later in uglier ways. People who over and over again take the martyr role gradually build internal resentments and hostilities which eventually surface and break out in many different ways, including psychosomatic illnesses, disproportionate rage or anger, overreaction, cynicism, the tendency to dump a lot of old stuff when provoked by some small weakness in another person, withdrawal or detachment, adopting an "I couldn't care less" attitude, and so forth. Dominant Dan and Dorothy Doormat marriages may appear on the surface to be harmonious, but they are sick and unhappy and mutually dissatisfying marriages.

Lose/win does not work any more than win/lose does. The only solution that will work over a period of time is win/win. It is the same principle taught by God in the conversion process. As we attempt to influence his other children toward his ways, we don't compel them to believe and think and live as we do. But neither do we capitulate to their beliefs, thoughts, and life-style. Instead we engage them in a mutual interaction process. We teach and testify in the spirit of love, which lubricates the processes of understanding in yielding new insights, even bringing to consciousness deeply buried spiritual impulses and imprints, even premortal awarenesses and agreements. (Testimony is as much one of recovery as discovery.)

Win/win is a total relationship philosophy. If we have a high emotional bank account with other people, we might make some unpopular win/lose decisions simply because of the time pressures or other practical realities that are present. And that's all right. Sometimes we must do this. But with such a large emotional bank account these small withdrawals won't put us into an overdrawn position. Perhaps later we might make new deposits by explaining why we made these difficult and unpopular decisions, or whatever. The key thing is that even though we may have to make some win/lose or lose/win decisions from time to time on fairly unimportant issues, we are continuously attempting to keep the relationship on a win/win basis by making new deposits into the emotional bank account.

Whenever people get into an overdrawn position on that account, the smallest win/lose decision can throw other things all out of proportion, greatly limiting our flexibility and freedom. With a huge emotional bank account we have much more flexibility, a far greater reserve capacity to draw upon, so that we can pretty well flow with what needs to be done on a moment-by-moment basis and not be unduly concerned about having every decision understood and liked.

When two win/lose people get together, that is, when two determined, stubborn, ego-invested individuals interact, the result will be lose/lose. Both will lose. The spirit of win/lose when attacked by win/lose creates a kind of vindictiveness, a desire to "get back" or to "get even," and it literally clouds one's judgment and blinds one's vision from the realization that murder is suicide, that revenge is a two-edged sword cutting both ways, and that in the last analysis no one and nothing can hurt us without our consent. Vengeance is that consent. "An angry man digs two graves."

Let's say you have a difference with your spouse or one of your children. Just try this three-step win/win approach.

First, say something to this effect: "Let's communicate until we can find a solution we both can feel good about. Would you be willing to do this?" (My experience is that unless the situation is one of a terribly overdrawn emotional bank account situation, you will almost inevitably get a yes to this question.)

Second, say to the other, in effect: "I would like to listen to you first. I would like to understand how you see it and how you feel about it." Then actually listen with a full intent to understand and not to reply. Listen with an open mind and an open heart.

Third, when you sense the other feels understood, express how you see it and how you feel about it with as much courage and conviction as you can actually feel. You will find that if you truly learned from the other person and understand how he or she sees it and feels about it, it won't necessarily change your perception and feeling but it will moderate the tone of your expression. That tone will be much more respectful and considerate. This is the very essence of maturity: to be able to *express your feelings and convictions with courage, balanced with consideration for the feelings and convictions of others.*

If people will follow these three simple steps (which really are three principles) in about that order, they will find that they can resolve most of the relationship differences and difficulties confronting them. It is when we violate these three principles by either starting with a win/lose or a lose/win attitude, or seeking first to be understood rather than to understand, that we will bring about ego investment into different positions. Then both parties will tend to think win/lose, get their defenses up, think in dichotomies (either/or), and close down their creative minds from generating different options which may have mutual benefit in them (win/win). Over time they will find that these differences will be exacerbated until they end up in what is typically called a personality conflict or a communication breakdown. But really, at bottom, they were only untended misunderstandings.

Look on it this way. If you suddenly went without air, what would happen to your interest in reading this book? As interested as you might be before that, you would lose all interest. Your dominant need is survival. Now that you have air and are not concerned about it, air doesn't motivate you at all. Rather, learning does. Similarly, when we listen to someone deeply and fully it is like giving him psychological air and it literally will take the sword right out of his hand. His defenses will lower, simply because he is not fighting anybody. He is accepted and someone is seeking to understand him. "Air" is being given to him, so it doesn't motivate him any longer. But just start seeking to be understood before he feels understood, or seek to get your way in spite of his opposing feelings, and it will be like taking air from him. The dominant motive will be to get that psychological air back—that feeling that I count, that I matter, that I am a person of worth, that I am to be respected and to be understood.

This doesn't mean that you agree with the other person, because agreement is a totally different matter from understanding. Most people fear giving understanding, thinking it will be perceived as a form of agreement. If you are concerned about that, make it very explicit what you are doing; that you are neither agreeing nor disagreeing, you are merely seeking to understand. But seek *sincerely* to understand. Such open-heartedness and open-mindedness will have its effect upon you, and you may really change. You may end up agreeing, or you may end up with an honest disagreement. But because you have paid the price in respecting the communication and the relationship, you will express that disagreement differently, with more reverence, with more humility, even though you may express it with courage and conviction. You simply disagree agreeably.

The Abundance Mentality

I hope you understand the principle of win/win at this stage, with an awareness that it is based upon the communication principle of seeking first to understand before seeking to be understood. Note too that it is based upon an emotional trait or capacity of what I like to call the abundance mentality. This basically means that you don't see life as a big competition, and that most of your psychic satisfactions don't come from winning through beating others or from being compared to others, either positively or negatively.

Most people develop the opposite of the abundance mentality—the scarcity mentality. They see life as a zero sum game—that if someone wins, someone else loses. They think in adversarial ways, in competitive ways. Perhaps in their childhood, love was given them on such a conditional basis and comparisons were so constant and controlling that their very view of life and of themselves is affected by all of that. With such a scarcity mentality the win/lose or the lose/win posture becomes a kind of psychological script they have learned. Transactional analysis people call it the "I'm okay, you're not okay" posture, or the "I'm not okay, you're okay" posture. In management and leadership theory, win/lose is called authoritarian or dictatorial, and lose/win is called permissive, laissez-faire, or nice-guy, country-club approaches.

Many people give lip service to the win/win ideal and even attempt to practice active listening, whereas they are merely putting new sheep's clothing on the old wolf. They use these attitudes and skills as manipulative ploys to get what they want. Fundamentally, deep inside, they define winning as defeating someone. They were too scripted by conditional love supplies in their childhood or during their teenage period, when acceptance and belonging to a group is based on comparisons and exclusions and the fraternity/sorority principle. Or perhaps they were deeply programmed and scripted by competitive athletics and began to see all of life through that filter. Inevitably, under stress the old wolf will throw off the sheep's clothing and his true heart will emerge. Win/win may be on the sweater, but win/lose remains on the heart.

That is, it does unless the heart is changed through a divine procedure called conversion; conversion to the win/win Personality of the universe. That Personality is one who does not make comparisons—who loves all of his children unconditionally and whose happiness, whose work and glory is completely interwoven with the happiness, growth, and development—eventually the eternal life—of his children; one who is willing to give all he has, as demonstrated in the giving of his Only Begotten Son; one who is willing to have us be co-inheritors of everything. When people get a new heart and mind and deeply sense the win/win principle, they have the correct perspective for establishing good communication/problem-solving systems and good stewardship/discipline systems.

Principles of Stewardship/Discipline

I suggest that a good stewardship/discipline system is a clear mutual understanding and commitment regarding expectations. Consider that phrase again: mutual understanding and commitment regarding expectations. Can you sense the spirit of win/win in that? Mutual understanding and commitment. These expectations would fall under five areas:

First, *desired results* (in other words, where do we want to end up and when?).

Second, *guidelines*. These guidelines are correct principles, important policies, and standardized procedures; no-no's, or things not to do, things which obviously have proven to be failure paths in the past.

Third, *resources* (human, financial, organizational, or technical) which can be drawn upon to help the steward accomplish the desired results within the guidelines specified.

Fourth, *accountability*. Accountability specifies when progress reports are to be made, together with what the criteria or standards of performance are to be in evaluating results. In other words, when we establish desired results we should also hammer out indicators or criteria that would illustrate those desired results being accomplished. These criteria are the essence of the accountability process. Accountability means that the steward accounts on his stewardship based upon the criteria he helped develop. In other words, self-evaluation. It does not involve evaluation by the boss, the parent, or the master, because their evaluation has already been built into the win/win agreement— particularly in the desired results section of that agreement.

Fifth, *consequences*. Consequences could be financial rewards, or psychic rewards such as recognition and appreciation, including the intrinsic reward of knowing "I have come through." They may also include larger stewardships. ("Well done, thou good and faithful servant; thou hast been faithful over a few things, I will make thee ruler over many things.") They may include opportunities for training and development, new assignments, different jobs, and so on. These consequences have both positive and negative sides to them and could be explicitly stated in the win/win agreement or merely be implicitly understood. In this way no one is using secret criteria by which to evaluate anyone else. Everything is up front and understood at the beginning. People can evaluate themselves, they can judge themselves, and they even can "fire" themselves if they know they are not meeting their agreed-upon expectations.

This entire approach to stewardship and discipline is a practical application of Joseph Smith's leadership philosophy, "I teach them correct principles and they govern themselves." Notice that the word *teach* is a present tense word. Teaching is a constant, ongoing process. And remember that we define teaching primarily as modeling and relating, secondarily as telling. *Correct principles* means natural laws or gospel principles or wise policies, guidelines, and so forth. Once people receive these correct principles by selecting goals in harmony with them, then they can also govern themselves and evaluate themselves by them. The role of the parent in this case is: 1) as a source of help; 2) as the person who receives the accountability and helps establish the next win/win agreement; 3) as the person who establishes helpful systems such as training, information, communication, compensation, and so on, to reinforce the win/win agreement. In fact, in the center of these four systems to be managed and led for a family could be put the words *Correct Principles*.

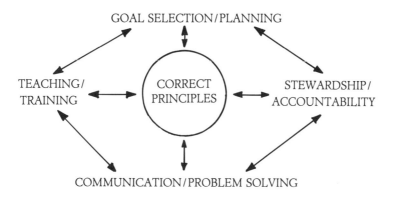

Green and Clean

In order to bridge the gap between this abstract theory and concrete reality, I would like to tell a true story about delegating a job to my son Stephen when he was only a little boy. This experience embodies the philosophy and the principles we have discussed in this stewardship/discipline system area. It is also a practical illustration of Joseph Smith's leadership philosophy quoted above: "I teach them correct principles and they govern themselves." The principles involved are put in parentheses, in the tone of an observer/teacher, following different parts of the story.

Twice a year—at the beginning of school and the beginning of summer—our family reorganizes the stewardships, or jobs, to be done. It usually takes two or three home nights and considerable teaching and training to complete the process. On a particular home night early in June, we wrote down on a large blackboard in our family room our family goals for that summer in light of our overall family goals. We also identified all of the important activities or stewardships which had to be done to accomplish these goals. Each member of the family volunteered to do particular jobs. For instance, I volunteered to make the money to pay for the mortgage, electricity, telephone, food, clothing, gasoline, and so on. My wife volunteered to have and take care of the babies. When it came to the different jobs no one wanted to do (called "yuk" jobs), we agreed to work out a system in which all who were capable of doing these jobs would take turns every few months.

My son Stephen volunteered for the yard stewardship. I agreed and defined the jobs in terms of two results, green and clean. (It is very important to define jobs in terms of desired results, not in terms of methods; then the delegatee feels the responsibility to do whatever is necessary to accomplish those desired results within the guidelines of correct principles.) "Son, your job is 'green and clean.' "

Then a two-week PC training process began. "Son, green is the color of our neighbor's yard." (Up to this time the yard stewardship was mine; I hadn't done all that well, so I needed my son to *see* a standard.) We went over to my neighbor's yard and looked at its color and I taught him that that color was a function of water. During the two-week training period, as we watered the lawn, he could *see* a relationship between correct watering and color. I also trained him in what clean meant. "Son, clean means that we don't have any paper or sticks or dog-leavings or rocks or whatever shouldn't be there. Now, son, let's clean up this half of the yard." Then we did the work together. "Good, son, I hadn't noticed that paper in the bush. Very good work.

"Now, son, look at the difference between the two halves of the yard. That half is clean, this half isn't." Then we cleaned the dirty half together. "Now let's go and do the same thing to the backyard, clean half of it and then see the difference." (All of this training was to establish a standard of performance, exactly what green and clean meant.)

After defining what green and clean meant, I told my son that it really didn't make any difference how he accomplished green and clean. I also told him that if he wanted to, I would tell him how I would do it. He asked me how I would do it and I answered, "I'd turn on the sprinklers, but if you want use the hose or buckets or spit all day long, it makes no difference. All I care about is green and clean."

About in the middle of the second week of training, I said to him, "Stephen, on Saturday I'm going to ask you if you will take the job. If you say yes, from then on it will be yours."

He said he was willing to take it right then.

I said, "No, son, I want you to think carefully what this means and what kind of work it involves. Let's keep working together, and you think about it, and then I'll ask you about it on Saturday morning." (It is important never to go too fast in establishing stewardships. There needs to be a process of understanding, of internalization, and it involves more than just intellectual understanding. It involves emotional understanding and emotional acceptance. The Savior said to his disciples, as recorded in Luke 14: "For which of you, intending to build a tower, sitteth not down first, and counteth the cost, whether he have sufficient to finish it. Lest haply, after he hath laid the foundation, and is not able to finish it, all that behold him begin to mock him, saying, This man began to build, and was not able to finish.''

We rehearsed again what green and clean meant. I told him that there were three other things that he needed to understand about the job before deciding to take it. The first was ''Who will be boss?''

He shrugged somewhat and said nothing.

I said, ''Son, you will be boss; you are in charge, you boss yourself.

''Second, son, guess who your helper will be.''

''Who, dad?''

''I will. I will be your helper. If you get into problems or have trouble or whatever, let me know and I will be happy to help. But you must realize, son, that many times I am away, and sometimes when I'm home I'm too busy doing other things and I won't be able to help. But whenever I have the time and whenever you need my help, you've got it. You boss me, you tell me what you want me to do.'' (It is important to identify yourself as a source of help, also to give some guidelines so that the requests for help are within reason.)

''Third, guess who judges your work, son?''

He said, ''Who?''

''You judge yourself. How do you think you judge yourself, son?''

He answered, ''Green and clean.''

''That's right, Stephen. What's green again, and what does clean mean?'' We agreed that twice a week we would walk around the yard together and he would show me how he was doing in his stewardship.

When Saturday morning came, I asked him if he was prepared to take the job. He said yes, so we rehearsed again exactly what this meant, what our agreement was.

''What is your job, son?''

''Green and clean.''

"What does green mean?... Clean?... Good, you understand. Who is your boss?"

"I boss myself."

"Who is your helper?"

"You are, if you have time."

"What if I don't have time?"

"My job is green and clean."

"Who judges you?"

"I judge myself."

"How do you judge yourself?"

"Green and clean."

"What's green?... Good. What's clean?... Good."

(This is called a win/win agreement. It involved a clear, mutual understanding and commitment to five things: desired results, guidelines, resources, accountability, and consequences. The consequence, really, was implicit, that is, satisfaction of having done what he agreed to do. But if necessary, I wouldn't have hesitated to make the consequences more explicit and tie it into privileges or making some money, which may have been necessary if he had been a little older.)

He was committed. All systems were "go."

He did nothing. He did nothing all that Saturday, Sunday, and Monday. It was a very hot June, the yard was becoming cluttered and just starting to yellow. I became concerned. I remember driving off to work on Tuesday morning and looking at "his" yard with some disgust, wondering what had happened. I rationalized away Saturday, we didn't work on Sunday, but I couldn't understand why he didn't work on Monday. So I was very anxious to see what would have taken place by Tuesday evening when I returned from work. I'll never forget driving around the corner, anxious to see the yard. Sure enough, nothing! Still cluttered, very dry, and starting to yellow—and my son Stephen was playing in the park across the street.

Frankly, I was ready to move to win/lose. (A win/lose job, an authoritarian job, would reverse almost all of the above-stated principles. It would focus on methods rather than results: "Turn on these sprinklers for thirty minutes, these for fifteen. Do this, do that." I would have been responsible to follow through, to judge, to reward or punish. There wouldn't have been very good feelings and the son wouldn't have grown very much, but the job might have gotten done.)

I was tempted to go for win/lose, because I was getting upset and I could feel a growing need for control and was disillusioned by his performance after two weeks of training and all those commitments. I had a lot of money invested in the yard and could see it going down the drain. Besides that, my neighbor's yard was manicured and beautiful, and the situation was getting downright embarrassing.

But I faked it. I tried to be pleasant. I shouted across the street to Stephen, "Hi, son, how ya doin'?"

He answered, "Fine."

"How's it going in the yard?"

He answered, "Fine."

By asking for an accountability in that way, I had just broken the mutual understanding we had achieved. We had agreed to walk around the yard and that he would show me how he was doing. So he felt perfectly justified in giving the accounting he had now given.

I bit my tongue and decided to say nothing until after dinner and then to walk around the yard with him. I had to reaffirm within myself that my primary purpose was his character development. The yard was only a means to that. I was really raising children, not grass.

So after dinner I said, "Son, why don't we walk around the yard and see how things are going, just as we had agreed?" We got out in the middle of the front yard and Stephen broke down and started to cry. His lip and chin started to quiver, and he barely said, "It's so hard."

Well, what was hard? He hadn't done one single thing. (What was hard was the exercise of initiative or self-governance. But this is also the essence of growth. If we nag the child, work becomes the course of least resistance, the easiest thing to do. But there is no growth in the course of least resistance.)

I responded, "Is there anything you would like me to do?"
He answered, "Would you?"
"You bet! What was our agreement?"
"You said you'd help if you have time."
"I have time."
"Just a minute, dad." He ran into the house and came out with two sacks. He handed me one and took one himself and said to me, "Would you clean up that over there?" He directed me in cleaning up the yard and gave me the worst part to do, including some strewn garbage on the side lawn. (Notice who was directing whom.) I did exactly as he asked, then held the sack. He took it and emptied it.

It was at that very moment I have just described that he signed the psychological contract, or the win/win agreement deep within himself. It then became his yard. He asked for help only two or three times that entire summer. It became a trust, a stewardship. He developed a great deal of pride around "green and clean." And he would get after his brothers and sisters if they threw stuff around out there.

I am convinced that if stewardships are set up correctly, based on high trust, considerable training, and mutual understanding of exactly what is expected; and if sufficient time is given for the steward to make a commitment; and if the delegator is sincere in his or her willingness to be a source of help as requested by the delegatee; and if both parties understand the accountability process, in that the steward judges his own performance (as took place in the parable of the talents or the parable of the pounds) — if these conditions are satisfied, then the stewardship will be properly established and executed and accounted for. If misunderstandings or problems arise, consider the agreement or contract open so that either party can discuss it again, clarify it, and perhaps renegotiate.

This approach involves an entirely new way of looking at delegation or establishing stewardships, in that it changes the nature of the relationships. The steward becomes his own boss, governed by a conscience that contains the commitment to certain desired results. It also releases the creative energies of that person in doing whatever is necessary in harmony with correct principles to achieve those desired results. The steward is further honored by judging himself rather than by having an outside judge. If the test is difficult, he'll be twice as hard on himself as the delegator would dare be.

What the delegator does do is carry out the agreed-upon consequences, consequences such as I outlined a few pages back.

The main problems most parents face with this approach are problems in ourselves, the parents. These are impatience, the unwillingness to pay the price in PC work (proper training), and hesitancy to change roles and become a helper instead of a boss, and particularly the reluctance to stop all nagging and to allow the other person to evaluate himself, based upon the criteria specified in the win/win agreement. Many people attempt to apply some of these ideas and techniques, but with the old authoritarian mindset. They inevitably find that their true perception and feeling surface and they end up nagging. Then they condemn the principles and philosophy, saying that it simply won't work, that it isn't geared to certain kinds of people, or whatever.

But the approach is entirely flexible and is adaptable to any kind of situation, with any kind of person. The story above dealt with a little boy, but remember that it will work with teenagers, immature adults, and mature adults, simply because there is so much *flexibility* in the five aspects of the psychological contract or win/win agreement. If people are immature, you'll have fewer desired results or more guidelines, identify more resources, have more frequent accountability and more immediate consequences. If people are more mature you will specify more challenging desired results, need fewer guidelines, have less frequent accountability, and have less measurable and more discernible criteria.

If you want a full discussion of all these principles, get hold of the teacher development manual put out several years ago by the Teacher Development Committee of the Church called *Super-*

vision in Teaching. This manual has the picture of the Prophet Joseph Smith on the front along with his leadership philosophy, "I teach them correct principles and they govern themselves." The basic principles in it are the principles which General Authorities have been counseling Regional Representatives to teach stake and ward priesthood leaders over the last several years. Because of organizational and title changes, *Supervision in Teaching* is no longer published, but you might find an old copy in ward or branch libraries or in the personal libraries of those who were once called to be teacher development directors. Literally tens of thousands of this manual were distributed in the late 60s and early 70s.

For twenty years now I have been teaching these principles and this philosophy in many different situations (family, Church, business, academic, government, and so on). I believe that wherever you find outstandingly successful results in terms of P/PC balance, high productivity or profits (or however that organization measures success), combined with the growth and development of the people and the culture, you will find this philosophy and these principles in operation, whether or not the words used are the same. It is the essence of the approach or philosophy of the outstanding companies in the United States and in Japan. The nonfiction best-seller *The Search for Excellence*, by Peters and Waterman, contains eight basic lessons of the best-run American companies and could almost be retitled "Teach Correct Principles and Let Them Govern Themselves."

I believe Joseph Smith's leadership philosophy to be the most comprehensive, the most progressive, the most down-to-earth and practical, the most individualistic, the most growth-producing, and the most results-producing in the long run of any philosophy ever enunciated. It is based upon eternal concepts and truths. I am absolutely convinced of this and see innumerable scientific studies verifying it. I also find the organizational world literally hungry for a philosophy based on correct maps

and principles. As Latter-day Saints we are fortunate beyond expression to have a correct map revealed to us of who man really
is, what his true potential is, and what are the correct principles
which govern his growth and happiness. And certainly there is no
setting as important or as much in need of the application of
these principles as the family setting.

26

Three Critical Skills in Producing, Managing, and Leading

Time management, communication, and problem solving are common denominator-type skills. That means they are needed in every phase of life and become critically important in marriage and family life. Perhaps the most marvelous feature of these three skills is that they are learnable. This means that improvement in these three skills lies within our own control. We can't do very much about other people's behavior, but we can do a great deal about our own, particularly in three areas: how we manage our time, how we communicate with others, and how we solve the problems and challenges of life.

Let's consider each skill in turn, one in this chapter and the other two in chapters 27 and 28.

Time Management

The title Time Management is really a misnomer, because all people have exactly the same amount of time, but we all know that some accomplish several times as much as others do with their time. *Self-management* is a better term, because it implies that we manage ourselves in the time allotted us.

Most people manage their lives by crises; they are literally driven by external events and circumstances and particularly by problems. They become problem minded, and the only real priority setting they do is between one problem and another.

Effective time managers are not problem minded; they are opportunity minded. This doesn't mean they deny or ignore problems; it means they starve them; they think preventively. They occasionally have to deal with acute problems or crises, but in the main they prevent them from reaching this level of concern through careful analysis into the nature of the problems and through long-range planning.

The essence of time management is to set priorities and then to organize and execute around those priorities. That is the bottom line of the whole subject—set priorities, then organize and execute around them.

If you were to attend the successful time-management seminars or read the extensive literature, I believe you would find that the whole subject area can be summarized in the one expression: *set priorities, then organize and execute around those priorities*. Almost all of the principles and practices taught in these various seminars and books are but appendages to that central theme.

Most of the time-management seminars teach a very simple approach to setting priorities—A, B, C; A standing for most important matters, B for those of middle importance, and C for those of little or no importance.

Many confuse importance with urgency, even equating the two. But they are fundamentally different ideas. Importance is effect on desired results. For instance, if one activity would have an overwhelming effect on desired results, that activity would be considered highly important, or at an A level of importance.

Urgency means that something needs quick action, or is insistent and appears to require that something be done about it.

A ringing phone has the appearance of needing quick action, someone to answer it. It is insistent. It is therefore urgent. But it may be very unimportant. In fact, in various time-management seminars, whenever people make lists of the time-wasters, at or near the top of most lists are unimportant phone calls or phone interruptions. Phone calls almost always take priority over face-to-face visits, and yet the person who took the time to make a personal visit to an office is eclipsed by a ringing phone with a caller who may have the same problem. Somehow it doesn't seem right, but we all know it happens constantly.

Once you clearly understand the difference between importance and urgency, a whole new, fresh way of thinking about time management emerges. It takes a while to think about this difference and to get it inside you so you can *feel* the difference as well. Most people have equated urgency with importance for so long and have cultivated almost the second nature or knee-jerk habit of responding to the urgent that they wouldn't even think to separate the two concepts, to attend to the important and to benignly neglect the urgent but unimportant. The same individuals then wonder why other people accomplish so much more than they. They feel that they are literally being bombarded by one problem or crisis after another and barely even have breathing space, let alone time for PC activities and for planning and deep, meaningful, one-on-one communication, for preparation, and for a number of other things, none of which are urgent but all of which are important.

This isn't just a matter of playing with words or with how words are defined (the field of semantics). It is a matter of playing with scripts, with deeply imbedded scripts which result in habits. Horace Mann once said, "Habit is a cable; we weave a strand of it every day of our life and soon it cannot be broken." Most people's scripts combine urgency and importance. They could rescript themselves through some of the ways presented in this and other material, particularly by relying upon the source of true scripts, the scriptures. This would give them an amazing sense of freedom, of liberation, of power to choose their own response in any given set of circumstances. They would come to realize that everything is a trade-off: if you say yes to that which is urgent but not important, you are in fact saying no to that which is far more important but less urgent. This is what the time-management people call the activity trap. People are trapped by one activity after another. They are busy to the hilt. They are scheduled like a war plant, but they seemingly accomplish very, very little.

One of the secrets is to learn to smile when we say no, because inwardly we're realizing we are saying yes to something far more important than that to which we are saying no. But people who lack discipline in organizing their lives around priorities cannot smile when they say no, because their alternative is not to give their energies in a proactive (that is, opposite of reactive) way toward opportunities and important but not urgent priorities. It's better to work on the urgent but relatively unimportant than to do nothing. That's why they can't smile about it; in fact, they'll feel laden with guilt about it.

Once while serving as the Director of University Relations for Brigham Young University, I hired a very competent, talented, proactive, creative writer. I remember that one day, after he'd been on the job for a few months, I went into his office and asked him to work on some urgent matters which were pressing upon us. He said he would be happy to do so, if that's what I desired. Then he took me to his wall board, on which he had listed over two dozen different projects he was working on, together with target dates and level of accomplishment indicated. Then he asked me to help him decide which ones to take down, slow down, or defer in order to satisfy my request. When I sensed how organized he was, how disciplined, and how important all those different projects were, I hesitated to move in on his life and working schedule, so I backed off and found someone else to do the work, one whose basic habit patterns were geared to crises and problems. The work I wanted done was relatively unimportant but it was very urgent.

In studying my own life I have found that if I don't have a clear conception of what I am about, of what the desired results are that I'm going after, it is easy to be diverted into responding to urgent tasks. Urgent matters are usually visible; they press on us; they insist on action. They're often popular with others. They're usually proximate, right in front of us like mail on a desk. And often they are very pleasant, easy to do, fun to do. But usually they are unimportant! Not always, however; sometimes the urgent is also the important and of course must then be attended to immediately. In spite of the best plans, there will always be emergencies and other unplanned-for events which will move in and require us to adapt, to be flexible, to reset priorities, and to organize and execute around those new priorities. But the principle remains the same; and we need to continually ask ourselves the question, "Is that which is pressing upon me now more important—not more urgent, but more important—than what I am doing?" If it is, let's have the courage to give our energies to it as soon as practical.

	URGENT	NOT URGENT
IMPORTANT	1	2
NOT IMPORTANT	3	4

Using the accompanying diagram, another way of putting this basic time-management philosophy is to substitute quadrants 3 and 4 for quadrant 2. In other words, until the "important" things are done, we shouldn't even work on the "not important" things, the unimportant things, such as those represented by quadrants 3 and 4. They may be pressing, popular, proximate, and pleasant, but if they are not important they should be neglected. We should smilingly say no to them; or if they have some importance, perhaps we should delegate them, or assign them a C rating and then handle them only after doing all the As and Bs. Perhaps if they are neglected, little by little they will go away; or perhaps they will become both urgent and important, so by delegating them initially to individuals who have those matters as their responsibilities we can be sure they will be taken care of, and we can then give our energies to the important matters which are our main responsibilities.

The Apostles said, "It is not reason that we should leave the word of God, and serve tables" (Acts 6:2). The Savior said to Martha, "Martha, Martha, thou art careful and troubled about many things: but one thing is needful: and Mary has chosen that good part." (Luke 10:41-42.) The scriptures are replete, almost page by page, with the principle of setting priorities. In fact, the essential thrust of the entire gospel message is a principle of setting priorities. The whole concept of the Ten Commandments, or of the two great commandments, or of the principles of consecration and stewardship and of putting God first and seeking first the kingdom of God, or the principle behind the Sabbath day, the study of scriptures, personal prayer—the entire concept of any of these could almost be subsumed under the topic "Set priorities."

I will never forget an experience with a Young Presidents Organization chapter in the East that invited my wife and me to put on a two-day seminar on developing a team spirit in the family. We attempted to teach many of the principles enunciated in this book—the concepts were the same, though we didn't use religious language. The seminar was proceeding fine, and by the end of the second day we opened it up for question and answer and problem solving. It then became increasingly apparent to the participants that the underlying problem, the root of most of the other problems we had been discussing for those two days, was that marriage and family life simply did not have a high-priority position with most of those who were present.

Remember that all these people were presidents of their own companies, or spouses of presidents. In order to crystallize the emerging consensus, in a special meeting for parents only (my wife was training the teenagers in communication skills) I confronted them as forcefully and directly as I felt I could with this kind of question: "If you had a new product you wanted to introduce which you felt had great potential, and you wanted to carry on a nationwide marketing program to do it, would that excite you? Would you do what was necessary to accomplish that? Or if you had a competitor move in on your territory and take away a sizeable hunk of your business, would you be determined to take immediate steps to remedy the situation? Or if one of your services or products was being unusually accepted in one test market and you had a two-year lead time on your competitors, would that turn your talents and energies on? Would you organize yourself to capitalize on that situation as far as you possibly could?''

Almost to a person, all the answers were in the affirmative. They knew what they needed to do, or if they didn't know they would soon find out. It would become a high priority item and they would organize their life to do whatever was necessary to accomplish the desired result. They would make sacrifices. They would put aside lesser projects. They would enlist others to give them help. They would bring to bear the full talent, expertise, experience, skill, wisdom, and dedication in doing whatever was necessary to make a success out of the project.

I then changed the line of reasoning and questioning to marriage and the family. If there had been any doubt before there was none now: it became clear—almost embarrassingly obvious to virtually everyone there—that the fundamental problem, the source of pretty well every other problem, was the low priority assigned to the family. Too many were looking for shortcuts, quick fixes—not life-style changes.

Setting priorities requires us to think carefully and clearly about values, about ultimate concerns. These then have to be translated into long- and short-term goals and plans, and translated once more into schedules or time slots. Then, unless something more important—not something more urgent—comes along, we must discipline ourselves to do as we planned.

"When we pick up one end of the stick, we pick up the other."

27

The Communication Skill

In order to do algebra, we must first understand basic math. This is the same reason why we study the communication skill before the problem-solving skill. Communication is a prerequisite to problem solving; it is the most fundamental and necessary skill in life.

Two Translations

Communication could almost be defined as mutual understanding. When two people truly understand each other, they have communicated. One of our Articles of Faith says, "We believe the Bible to be the word of God as far as it is translated correctly." The main problem in communication is the translation problem. In fact, two translations take place in communication. The first one consists in translating what we mean into what we say; the second one requires the listener to translate what we say into what we mean. The first challenge, therefore, is to learn to say what we mean; the second challenge is to learn to listen so that we understand what others mean.

"I know you think you understand what I said, but I'm not sure you understand that what I said is not what I mean."

Let's look deeper into the translation problem. We all live in two worlds—the private, subjective world inside our heads, and the real, objective world outside. We could call the former, personal maps, and the latter, the territory. None of us has an absolutely complete and perfect map of the territory, or the real, objective world. Science itself is in a constant state of evolving better and better maps. Only the creator of the territory has the complete, perfect map, and to the degree that our map does match the territory we possess truth. As we discussed before, citing the Lord's definition of truth, "Truth is *knowledge* of things as they are, and as they were, and as they are to come." (D&C 93:24. Italics added.)

Most of us are too filled with our own autobiography—that is, our own maps of the world, of the way things are to us and the way things should be to us. We have the tendency to listen to others autobiographically—that is, through our autobiography, through our maps, our own personal frame of reference, and our word definitions.

When we listen autobiographically rather than empathetically (meaning, from the point of view of the one communicating), we fall into the translation trap. In my mind, without a doubt the number one problem in the field of communication is that *most people do not really listen with the intent to understand; rather, they listen with the intent to reply.* Even while we are listening (or reading) there is an internal self-talk process going on. We take what we hear and compare it with what we know, then prepare to give our evaluative reply or response.

Instead we should strive first to be a more accurate translator. When someone is attempting to translate a foreign language to an audience, he isn't attempting to evaluate or judge what is being said but is striving to be faithful in communicating the true intent and content of the speaker. He sees himself more as a vessel or a vehicle than as an evaluator or editorializer or commentator; that is, if he is a good translator and faithful to his task.

The problem is that in marriage and family life we are so emotionally invested in the issues, we care so terribly about what is happening, and our feelings are so strong, that we lose the cool, objective detachment which a faithful translator possesses. We are simply too full of ourselves, too full of our autobiography. When the issues are emotionally charged we are most vulnerable. Then listening is risky business; deep genuine listening is very, very risky. We risk being influenced, we risk being changed, we risk being wrong, we risk losing control, we risk losing a feeling of certainty and predictability. We're not sure what Pandora's box will be opened up, we're not sure where we're going to end up.

To listen deeply and genuinely to another on issues that affect our lives takes an enormous amount of internal personal security. This is because if we are changed as a result, if we are influenced, we need to be able to say, "So what?" It makes no real difference, because down deep we are changeless; down deep there is a core set of values and feelings which represent the real self. At this core there is a sense of intrinsic worth which is independent of how others treat us, including spouse or children. This is our inviolate self, our true identity. Nowhere is it more true than in marriage and family life that when we are invulnerable down deep we can afford to be open, influenceable, teachable, and good listeners on the surface; but nowhere is it more true than in marriage and family life that when we are vulnerable down deep we can least afford to be open and influenceable and teachable and good listeners. This is the case simply because we are so invested and the issues are so emotionally laden.

For if my security lies in my opinions, what happens to me when my opinions are questioned, perhaps even proven incorrect? Where else can I go, where do I then run and hide? The person who acts as if he doesn't really care about other people's opinions is wearing a mask. In most cases, such a person cares too much. He is simply too vulnerable to other people's opinions; he can't afford to listen to them or he may be wiped out. A person protects himself from exposing this soft, tender, vulnerable center by acting as if he doesn't care, by pretending invulnerability.

Secure people care about others' opinions so as to be effective with them, but they don't derive their security from them.

Two Levels: Technique and Security

I hope it has become clear that we must look at the communication skill as we would at an iceberg—at two levels. The small, visible part of the iceberg is the skill or technique level of communication. The great mass of the iceberg, silent and unseen beneath the surface of the water, represents the deeper level, the attitudinal, motivational level. Let's call it one's security base. To make any significant long-term improvement in our communication abilities requires us to work at both levels, technique and security. Of the two, the security level is the most basic and needful and therefore the most important. Yet it isn't all that is important. Skill with technique plays a major role and can even assist in cultivating and deepening the security base. Seven specific ways on how to develop this security base—that is, a sense of intrinsic worth and security—are discussed at the end of this book, but also everything else we are saying about communication either implicitly or explicitly builds on this security base.

Perception

Before targeting in on the two main communication skills, empathic listening and authentic sharing, there are four other fundamental ideas important to the understanding of communication. First, the idea of *perception;* second, *brain dominance theory;* third, *the three channels of communication;* and fourth, *the trust level,* or what we've been calling the emotional bank account. Let's look at each in turn.

First, perception. Perception merely means that all of us see the world through the filter or lens of our own experience, scripts, maps; in other words, *we see the world as we are, not as it is,* and we can only act out of what we see and understand. When a person truly understands this idea it will change his manner of speech. Instead of saying, "This is the way it is," he will say, "This is how I see it." Instead of saying "It's," he will say "In my view" or "In my opinion" or "As I see it." His language will be garnished with humility and reverence rather than arrogance or cocksureness. Such an attitude gives psychic space to other people, allows them the feeling that they can express how they see something and how they feel about something. Otherwise they would feel that if they saw and expressed it differently from someone else, they would probably have an ugly confrontation of some kind. Such a manner of speech born of genuine humility literally admits other people to the human race. It says to them: "You matter too. Like mine, your views and feelings are legitimate and need to be respected." Otherwise, they would feel: "If he is right and I feel differently, then I must be wrong. But to me I'm right. I'm confused."

Similarly, when others judge or condemn or disagree with us, our manner of speech and reply will be like the following in tone, if not in language: "Good, you see it differently. I would like to understand how you see it." That's instead of, "You're wrong and I'm right." Then when we disagree with another, instead of saying, in effect, "I'm right and you're wrong," we will say, "I see it differently. Let me share with you how I see it."

The Savior taught: "Agree with thine adversary quickly, whiles thou art in the way with him; lest at any time the adversary deliver thee to the judge, and the judge deliver thee to the officer, and thou be cast into prison. Verily I say unto thee, Thou shalt not come out thence, till thou hast paid the uttermost farthing." (Matthew 5:25-26.)

Whenever we are "so right" as to make everyone who sees and thinks differently feel wrong, their best protection from further injury from us is to label us, to peg us, to put us behind mental and emotional bars and walls for an indeterminate jail sentence, and we will not come out until we pay the uttermost farthing. That is the farthing of humility, of acknowledging honestly our wrong, our unkindness, our injustice, or whatever, and of permitting the other person to enter the human race—that is, giving legitimacy to his identity and views and feelings.

The relative success which the marriage encounter movement throughout the country has had is largely attributable to couples having been trained to adopt the above attitude and to listen to each other empathetically and restate their understanding of what was meant until mutual understanding or communication is achieved. The couple starts with safe, peripheral issues and differences and gradually moves toward the more tender, vulnerable areas; just as an athlete might purposely handicap himself in some way during the *safe* preparation phase in order to release the full potential without that handicap in the real-life phase; just as, according to report, Demosthenes, the great Greek orator, would fill his mouth with beach pebbles until he could speak distinctly and clearly in that *safe* environment; or just as a quarterback might palm basketballs or even medicine balls in order to strengthen the hand and forearm muscles in order to become relatively independent of the size or weight or degree of wetness of the football snapped to him in the game.

President Heber J. Grant was fond of quoting Emerson: "That which we persist in doing becomes easy; not that the nature of the thing has changed, but that our ability to do has increased." As people communicate back and forth, starting with small, safe issues and moving to the larger, tougher issues, they develop the emotional muscles needed for serious problem-solving in their marriage and family life.

Brain Dominance Theory

Brain dominance theory, mentioned previously, has great relevance in the field of communication. The more we attempt to appreciate and use both the logical and verbal left brain and the intuitive, sensing, feeling, creative right brain, the more we can adapt to the other person's mode of communication and truly empathize. The language of logic and the language of sentiment are simply two different languages, and of the two the language of sentiment or emotion is far more motivational and powerful. This is why it is so important to listen primarily with our eyes and heart, and secondarily with our ears.

The most significant part of communication is nonverbal, because that part communicates intent; the verbal part communicates content. In short, we must strive to communicate as a whole person listening to a whole person.

Three Channels of Communication

The three basic channels of communication are words, sounds, and body (facial expression, gestures, body posture). The context or physical environment, the distance between people, and so on, become other important factors. Communication experts estimate that, over the long run, of the three channels spoken of, words alone carry only a third of the power and influence of sounds, and sounds only half of the power and influence of body language. In other words, words represent about 10 percent of communication, sounds 30 percent, and body language 60 percent.

Test it for yourself, if you wish. Looking in another direction than at your spouse and without any warmth or inflection in your voice, just say the words, "I love you." Then add warmth and feeling to the sound of those words, and you will both clearly sense the difference between words alone and the added effect of tone or sound. Then throw your whole face and arms and body into it and express your love. You will observe the substantial difference between the effects of words, sounds, and body language. Now, use only body language with no words, and you will discover the relative unimportance of words.

In the last analysis it is what we are that communicates far more eloquently than what we say. The body simply does not lie. There are too many subtle, hidden cues that come across. Over time our true feelings communicate, regardless of our best efforts to mask them. This is why the most fundamental way to improve our communication is simply to improve ourselves as people, to become more vital and loving and integrated.

Trust Level

All of this is the essence of what our fourth idea is about, that is, *the emotional bank account* or trust level. Again, you can test it easily for yourself. Think of someone with whom you have an extremely high emotional bank account, a high trust level. Can you not communicate with them almost without words? Can you not even make mistakes in your verbal communication and still find that they get your meaning? On the other hand, think of other people where the trust level is low. Don't you find that it really makes little difference how hard you try to communicate or how good you are in technique or how clear your language is?

When trust is high, communication is easy, effortless, instantaneous, and accurate. When trust is low, communication is extremely difficult, exhausting, and ineffective. The key to communication is trust, and the key to trust is trustworthiness. Living a life of integrity is the best guarantee of maintaining the climate of effective communication. As in all natural processes, there are no shortcuts, no quick fixes. This is hard doctrine, yet it is glorious doctrine because it emancipates us from the myth and the illusion that there are shortcuts, that we can violate the law of the harvest and still make it.

Empathy

All of this finally leads us to the two basic skills of communication: (1) empathic listening, or listening for understanding; and (2) authentic sharing, or learning to say what we really feel and mean. Here are a few suggestions on each topic.

First, empathy. Strive to transcend your autobiography. That is, move out of yourself and into the mind and heart of others so that you can see the world as they see it. This does not mean that you feel as they feel. That is called sympathy. It means that you *understand* how they feel, based on how they see the world. That is empathy. Many people confuse empathy and sympathy and get into deep trouble doing so; namely, by leading people to believe that they are being agreed with rather than only being understood. Most people have had such little experience with being deeply understood that they often interpret any genuine listening as a sympathetic response, or agreement with what they are saying and feeling. When they later discover that was not so, their expectations are blasted, and they usually become more difficult than ever to communicate with, feeling that they have been led down the primrose path and been taken advantage of. Sometimes they will simply refuse to open up again.

This is why it is important to make it clear, explicitly clear if necessary, that you are not making any effort to evaluate, to agree or to disagree, but that your entire focus is only to understand, to see it as the other person sees it, and to understand how he feels. Strictly speaking, you will never fully see it as he sees it, but you'll try. Your attitude is: "I am trying to understand you. I may never understand, but I am going to try." Such an attitude is enormously attractive and appealing because it keeps you open, and others feel that you are learning, that you are influenceable. Remember that the key to your having influence with them is their perceiving that they have influence with you. But when you come to feel that you do understand, at that very moment you tend to become more closed; and in spite of efforts to mask such a posture, you send forth a subtle radiation, and others feel, "He thinks he understands, but he really doesn't." That you understand is really not as important as the continuing effort to understand. We're dealing with a dynamic, changing reality, not a static one.

Literally scores of times I have had this happen to me, particularly with members of my own family. They have said to me, behaviorally if not verbally, in essence: "I know what you're doing, daddy. I know you're trying to empathize with me, you're trying to listen to me, but you're not really listening at all. You really don't know where I'm coming from and what I'm really feeling." In many cases all I could do was acknowledge that was indeed the case. I was acting as if I understood, but I really didn't, and the difference between the two is perhaps only a little less than 180 degrees. Full and active listening takes courage to carry the risk of openness and the commitment to supply the energy needed to stay in the process.

After striving to transcend or rise above your own autobiography and get into the heart and mind of another, check out the accuracy of the understanding you have achieved by reflecting your understanding back of what the person is saying, and more importantly what he is feeling or meaning.

This doesn't mean mimicking or parroting another's words. Such mimicry insults people. They often wonder, "What is wrong with the way I'm saying it?" In fact, when you are sure you understand what another person means and you are sure that he feels you understand, you may not need to say anything at all, but rather to just keep on listening. But if you're not sure the other feels understood, or if you're not sure you do understand, check it out, test it with such words as: "I hear you saying"; "In other words, you feel"; "What I sense you mean is"; and so forth.

You have to be very up front and honest about this approach and must not be manipulative or "techniquey," particularly with those who know you well. Make it explicit what you are trying to do. Tell the other person that you are trying to empathize with him, that you are trying to reflect what you sense he means, and that you are not sure you understand so you are checking it out. People who know you well will just about demand such up-front honesty. If they don't get it, they might be rather suspicious of your reflective listening techniques, wondering what is going on, saying inside themselves: "I wonder what he is trying to do? He has never listened to me before." Or they may think, "Is he reading a book on active listening, or is he attending a seminar on marriage communication and then practicing his skills on me? But I know what he's really like." When you're up front, communicating clearly what your intention is, it defuses such cynicism and suspicion.

True and empathic listening is so powerful that I am constantly shocked at its influence. It is truly a miracle principle. If I were again to summarize in one sentence the single greatest learning of twenty years of study in this field, it would be, Seek first to understand, *then* to be understood. If the other feels understood, he is then best able and most desirous to understand you.

Authentic Sharing

After empathy, the second most vital communication skill is to *learn to say what we mean,* so that the other can understand. Frankly, if we truly empathize first, this becomes relatively easy to do. The key is to be in touch with our inmost feelings and true opinions and to give "I" messages. "I feel. . . ." "In my opinion. . . ." "As I see it, . . ." On the other hand, "you" messages—"Why are you so stubborn?" "You're so insensitive"—only stir up defenses and spawn the translation problems already discussed.

How this authentic sharing skill is developed and applied is discussed, mostly implicitly, in chapters 28 and 29. Little explicit attention is given to it, since I am convinced of the power and value of empathy in cultivating it and in dealing with *both* translation problems.

Suffice it to say, in conclusion to this chapter on communication, that if you want to be effective in presenting your point of view, start by demonstrating a good understanding of the alternative points of view. Articulate them better than their advocates can. Then share yours clearly and as forcefully as you wish, but with respect and humility.

28

The Problem-Solving Skill

In one sense, the only real test of our communication skill comes in interactive problem solving. Problems are simply real-life situations which are not the way people think they should be.

The classic approach to problem solving essentially deals with four questions: (1) Where are we? (2) Where do we want to go? (3) How do we get there? (4) How will we know we have arrived?

The first question—Where are we?—focuses on the importance of gathering and diagnosing reality data. The second question—Where do we want to go?—deals with clarifying values and selecting goals. The third question—How do we get there?—involves generating and evaluating alternatives, making a decision, and planning the action steps to implement it. The fourth question—how will we know we have arrived?—involves setting up criteria or standards to measure or observe or discern progress toward our objectives or goals.

When problems are emotionally charged up, as they often are in marriage and family situations, most people make assumptions about questions one and two, then begin to argue and fight over question number three. This only compounds the problem and increases people's emotional investment in what they want, cultivating the scarcity mentality; and they begin to define winning as defeating someone, to think in terms of dichotomies, or either/or approaches, and to go for win/lose solutions. As previously stated, when both parties have this win/lose attitude, then lose/lose is almost inevitable. Sometimes one of the parties will feel overpowered or intimidated and take up a lose/win position, but this will result in only temporary peace or resolution of the problem, with far more serious problems downstream.

What we want is a win/win solution wherein both parties feel good about it and feel committed to the decision and action plan. To achieve this takes more than time; it takes patience, self-control, courage balanced with consideration. In short, it takes considerable maturity and the exercise of our higher faculties.

Importance of Valuing Differences

Fundamental to win/win problem solving is the principle of valuing differences, as discussed in the material on the leader role. Immature people, on the other hand, strive to clone people, to make people over in their own image, to go for Professor Higgins's rhetorical question: "Why isn't a woman more like a man!" Yet it is in these very differences that the real strength in the relationship is found. We all know that in marriage this is so physically. Physical differences between men and women not only enable the reproduction of the human race and unity and fulfillment in other ways, but also teach us that oneness or unity does not mean sameness but rather complementariness. Of equal value to physical differences are mental and emotional differences. However, one with a scarcity mentality interprets these differences as the main problems or the main weaknesses in the marriage and the family, and somehow he or she feels it takes something away from self to acknowledge, accept, and value these differences. Not so with the abundance-mentality person. To him, differences are strengths, and they bring into play man's higher powers and faculties in order to create a complementary team based on mutual respect.

In addition to evidence from nature, many other illustrations could be developed from our other three models—Christ, the Church, and the temple—in pointing out the importance of valuing differences. The Godhead is composed of three separate personages, all with the same goal but different roles. The Church obviously is an interdependent institution in which different talents are obviously needed and appreciated. "For all have not every gift given unto them; for there are many gifts, and to every man is given a gift by the Spirit of God" (D&C 46:11). And the temple clearly teaches the complementary nature of the roles of man and woman and gives many explicit and implicit acknowledgements of dedicating differing talents to the Lord's cause. These divine sources or models give us true scripts regarding the value of differences. Too much of the world teaches false scripts, implying that equality lies in sameness. Clearly, in major respects "anatomy *is* destiny."

The very physical union of man and woman in marriage is a true scripting model of the principle that strength lies in differences. As the partners become one flesh, the marriage covenant itself is renewed and the divine mindset that "all things unto me are spiritual" (D&C 29:34) can become internalized and understood. As both parties turn to the Lord and each other with all their hearts in renewing the marriage covenant, it becomes sanctifying.

All of this does not mean that we do nothing about problems or differences. Instead it means that we value differences in order to solve problems. It means that we value the intrinsic worth of each person and the fact that each person does see and feel differently, and that in the process of genuine sharing and empathic listening the problems may be solved or transcended.

Resolving Differences

I would like to mention two books which have had enormous influence on my thinking with regard to problem solving and are very much in harmony with revealed spiritual principles. One book teaches us how to successfully confront and resolve differences, and the other one, how to successfully resolve differences by transcending them.

The first book, written by two Harvard law professors, Fisher and Ury, and entitled *Getting To Yes,* is an effort to present an alternative to the adversarial approach in law by employing the gentler arts of win/win negotiation. In this extremely helpful, practical book on principled negotiation, four basic principles are emphasized: first, separate the person from the problem; second, focus on interests, not positions; third, invent options for mutual gain; and fourth, insist on objective criteria.

Of the four, the first principle is obviously the most difficult to apply, but unless it is applied the other three principles cannot be. When we separate the person from the problem, we give legitimacy to people's differing perceptions and feelings. This enables us to listen to them in an effort to understand what their concerns, goals, and interests are. When people are unable to separate the person from the problem, then their focus is on positions and they tend to go either for win/lose or lose/win; minds become closed, defensive, and incapable of creating new options or alternatives which offer mutual gain or mutual benefit. Defensive minds simply are not creative; defensive minds think in dichotomies or "either/or" propositions—"If I'm right, you're wrong." The purpose of insisting on objective criteria is an effort to apply some well-established traditions or socially approved standards in order to have some kind of external evaluation of the decision. *Getting To Yes* is an outstanding little book full of clarifying illustrations and practical suggestions, and I recommend it to any married couple, or for that matter any family in the midst of sticky problems.

The other book was written by an English economist-philosopher, E. F. Schumacher, and is entitled *A Guide for the Perplexed.* In this brilliant little volume are many helpful, practical insights regarding the nature of problems and the unique qualities possessed only by human beings. Schumacher teaches that man's unique endowment is his self-awareness, which he defines as reflective thinking, or the ability to think about our thought processes. Animals can think, he says, but they can't think about their thinking and thereby step in on themselves and make changes (or rescript themselves, as we have been discussing in this book). Without agency they are essentially programs, not programers.

Schumacher teaches that there are two types of problems, convergent and divergent. Convergent problems (solved or unsolved) are capable of being solved by fact gathering and logical thinking processes. An illustration would be a design problem or a mechanical car problem. In principle, if we applied enough time, talent, and money in diagnosing the problem, gathering facts, and testing alternative solutions, we would be able to come up with a correct solution. Ultimately all approaches would converge toward a correct solution. Why? Simply because the thinking process complies with the laws of nature—laws at the level of inanimate nature.

But as soon as we move to the human level, as in marriage and family life, where people have differing perceptions, priorities, values, and philosophies—in short, different scripts—we confront a different type of problem, which Schumacher calls divergent. Very capable people may study such problems and come up with answers that contradict each other, answers that diverge from each other rather than converge. The more the problem is clarified and logically developed, the more the possible solutions will appear to be the exact opposite of each other. Schumacher argues against attempting to solve these problems in the traditional sense. He argues against seeking final solutions. Instead such problems, in order to be resolved, must be transcended— that is, a higher value or a higher principle needs to be brought into play. Schumacher comments: "I do not know who coined the slogan of the French revolution; he must have been a person of rare insight. To the pair of opposites, *Liberté* and *Egalité*, irreconcilable in ordinary logic, he added a third factor or force— *Fraternite, brotherliness—which comes from a higher level."* (A Guide *for the Perplexed*, Harper and Row, 1977.) In other words, the higher value of love transcends the diverging values of liberty and equality in such a way as to enable them to exist side by side.

Perhaps the classic illustration of such a divergent problem in our theology is the justice/mercy struggle. The principle of justice contains no mercy, and if we attempted to make it show mercy we would do away with justice. Justice and mercy are irreconcilable in logic, but we can transcend or rise above this diverging problem and draw down a value or principle from a higher level called repentance. This enables mercy and justice to be fused and each to play its proper role. Mercy cannot rob justice, but the combination of the principle of repentance and Christ's infinite atoning sacrifice has met the conditions of justice, and mercy is therefore received by those who repent and obey the laws and ordinances of the gospel. (See Alma 42.) Justice is thereby satisfied and the plan of mercy made efficacious.

Illustration: A Fishing Trip

To apply this thinking to a marriage, we could deal with any number of everyday practical problems wherein the solutions diverge from each other. For instance, let's say the husband wants to take his boys fishing during his summer week vacation and has been planning on it for several months. He's made reservations at a lake cottage and also arranged to rent a boat. His wife had also planned to go, but recently her aging mother has became ill and now she prefers to spend their week's vacation near her mother, about 250 miles away.

The husband argues: "The plans are set. The boys are excited. We should stay with our original plan."

The wife answers: "We don't know how much longer my mother will be around, and I want to be by her. This is our only opportunity to have enough time to do that."

The husband responds: "All year long we've looked forward to this one-week vacation. We'd be miserable sitting around grandmother's house for a week; besides she's not that sick. And she has another daughter nearby to take care of her."

The wife answers: "It's my mother, and I want to be with her myself."

The husband: "You could phone her every night. We're planning to see her at the Christmas family reunion anyway."

The wife: "That won't be for five more months, and how do you know she will be around for that long? Besides, she needs me and she wants me."

The husband: "She's being well taken care of. Besides, the boys and I need you too."

She: "My mother is more important than fishing."

He: "Your husband and sons are more important than your mother."

They end up quoting scriptures to each other to support their separate positions.

In this situation they're handling a divergent problem with convergent minds—it's like playing tennis with a golf club. The problem situation is larger than logic, and the best they'll come up with is some kind of compromise which will be unsatisfying to all—such as splitting up the family so that he takes the boys fishing and she visits her mother. If they did that, during the entire week both would feel guilty and unhappy. The sons would sense this and it would affect their enjoyment on the vacation. On the other hand, if the husband gave in to the wife, he would do so grudgingly and during the week away would consciously or unconsciously produce evidence to fulfill his prophecy of how miserable it was going to be for everybody. If she gave in to him, she might be very withdrawn and overreactive to any new developments about her mother which she learns on the phone. And, if the mother became seriously ill and died, the husband might never forgive himself—and the wife might not forgive herself (or him!) either.

Compounding the marriage problem may be the hurt feelings of the mother, judgments of the sister who has lived near the mother and has attended to her needs for such a long period of time without any respite, and comments of other family members about the whole situation.

The whole incident could become a major negative experience in the memory of this couple and family that might be rehearsed over the years as evidence of insensitivity, neglect, or incorrect priorities. It could be a source of contention for years and could even polarize a family.

Once a husband and/or wife put a judgment or label or peg on each other, they will begin to interpret most every event in terms of that judgment in order to validate it. The children may get in the middle of the crossfires. Torn and confused, the children may take it personally, even condemning themselves. Or they may take sides and compound the problem even further.

Many marriages that once were beautiful and soft and spontaneous and loving have deteriorated to the level of hostility through a series of incidents just like the one propounded above. The spouses simply acted out old conflicting scripts and used conflicting problem-solving strategies in the process. Divergent problems simply are not amenable to logic.

Synergistic Problem Solving

How then could such a problem be solved? It simply wouldn't be solved in the traditional sense. It would have to be grappled with, then eventually transcended by bringing into play higher principles and values. This is the essence of synergy, or synergistic problem solving. This requires that the husband and the wife, because their love for each other is greater than the desire to have their own way, become very open to each other's influence, communicate in depth, and come to really understand how each one sees the situation and feels about it. They would assure each other that their highest desire is to do what is right (a spirit of "Thy will, not mine, be done"), to do the Lord's will in this new circumstance, and to optimize the situation in such a way that everyone in the family has a happy, pleasant, even inspiring memory about that particular vacation week.

For instance, they may end up searching for alternative fishing areas near the grandmother's home. Or they might try to involve their cousins and work out some enjoyable joint-family activities along with good visits with the grandmother. Any number of other alternatives might be explored, such as finding out how ill the grandmother really is and arranging to have the wife spend time with her *after* the vacation. Or they might change altogether the nature of the recreational activity, even working it out so that the grandmother could join in in some way if her health permitted. Or if she were critically ill, they could all go and visit her and change altogether the purpose of their vacation, making it more of a family and spiritual time—thereby teaching a powerful lesson to the sons—and then working out side fishing trips later.

There are simply innumerable alternatives that can be explored when people have the mind to. Synergistic problem solving means creative problem solving. Our minds are enormously creative if we have the will to think about what we might do to find a solution which would truly be win/win. Synergy means that the whole is greater than the sum of its parts; that one plus one equals three or more.

Convergent thinkers tied to the logic of their own scripts will at best only compromise. Compromise is a very low form of win/win. Admittedly, in low-trust situations—overdrawn emotional bank accounts—it may be the only realistic one. But if deposits can be made into the bank account and the trust level increased, the parties can move towards synergistic solutions, or win/win at an extremely high level.

Synergistic solution means that through genuine two-way communication you come up with a solution that is better than any of the originally proposed solutions, and that both parties know this, feel it, and wouldn't hesitate to express it fully. It is simply a better solution and it came through the interaction; it came because of the relationship between the two people. The whole is more than the sum of its parts—it contains the relationship between the parts. "Only by persuasion, by long-suffering . . . by love unfeigned; by kindness, and pure knowledge. . . ." (D&C 121:41-42).

Let's say the couple came up with the solution of traveling to the grandmother's city and spending a great deal of time with her, but also had two or three days' fishing in a nearby lake. Let's also say that the fishing and the beauty of the surroundings wasn't nearly as good as those in the originally planned trip would have been. But they spent a lot of time with aunts, uncles, and cousins and had some other fun-filled activities. They got very close to their grandmother and she shared a lot of her life story with them. This would be a far superior solution to either of the original ones proposed, simply because of the *higher active principle of love.*

If he had his way and his wife went on the originally planned fishing vacation, the husband, sensing how badly she wanted to be with her mother, wouldn't really be happy. If she had her way and the family spent the week with the grandmother, she wouldn't be happy, knowing how disappointed her husband and children were in using their one-week vacation sitting inside four walls only out of a sense of duty.

Both of them would know that the new solution was better; they would both feel better about it; it would definitely be win/win.

Some excellent illustrations along this line are given in the book *Getting To Yes.* Two people are fighting over an orange, only to discover, when they really listen to each other, that one wants the peelings for a particular purpose and the other one wants the pulp to eat. In an office, one worker wants the window open, the other wants it closed. They could become adamant and defensive and thereby develop a bad spirit. Instead they separate the person from the problem, and both try to understand what the other person's interest are. One wants the window open in order to have fresh air, the other wants it closed to prevent the draft from blowing his desk papers about. They transcend this divergent problem by drawing upon a higher value or principle: that is, that the social or human environment is really more important than the physical environment. Their creative minds generate new alternatives and they finally settle on opening the window in the next room so that they have the fresh air without the draft. This is a better solution than either of the originally proposed ones, simply because part of their satisfaction in their working environment is how well they relate to each other. So they care about each other's feelings and listen to each other openly and sincerely.

The spirit of creative or synergistic problem solving is exciting. It's exciting because it's an adventure—neither of you knows where you are going to end up. All you do know is that you will end up better than where you are now.

The Daily Cross

"And he said to them all, if any man will come after me, let him deny himself, and take up his cross daily, and follow me" (Luke 9:23). I would like to suggest a particular interpretation of the Savior's teaching about our daily cross. This interpretation, in a sense, would synthesize this entire book at the practical level of problem solving.

I suggest that the cross we need to carry daily in our marriages and families is handed to us when we think we are literally at the end of our rope, when we are most exhausted, when things are most contradictory, difficult, and frustrating. It is then, *just then*, that life really makes sense. Such a circumstance provokes us, almost forces us, to develop our higher faculties. Until that point is reached, old scripts may have operated well for us. But when that point is reached they falter. They are simply inadequate. And because we are self-aware beings—beings who in a sense can stand apart from ourselves and observe our own thought processes, our scripts—it is at that very moment that we can choose to follow the Savior, to follow our model, to follow a new divine script. It is at that moment that our dormant spiritual muscles are awakened, exercised, and developed.

Such a moment comes in a marriage relationship when both parties have come to the end of their tether. Visualize this situation: "He is completely wrong and bull-headed and I am absolutely right, and I know it; and anyone else with any decency or reasonableness would know it too." It is at *that very moment* that a cross is being handed to us. If we strive to follow Christ, to handle the situation as we feel he would want us to, we would exercise our higher faculties and partake more of the divine nature. (Study 1 Peter 1.)

Mentally rehearsing beforehand through visualization and prayer can help us prepare to handle such moments. It is then that the scriptures we have pondered, even memorized, come to our consciousness, and the Spirit will tell us what we should do. (Study 2 Nephi 31-32.) Whenever we are out of our comfort zone, old scripts are completely inadequate. We must depend upon our new model, Christ himself. And if we have truly studied his ways and emotionally identified with him, his personality, his purposes, his church, his home, his thought processes, his reactions in different situations, and if we all are open to the Spirit, his Holy Spirit, then we will receive divine guidance. Such is the spiritual adventure.

Every time we yield to the upward temptation, the strength of that divine pattern is absorbed or scripted into our character. Every time we yield to the lower temptation, strength is taken from our character and the old script is welded more firmly into place. Marriage and family life is the supreme environment wherein these tests will come most continuously and fully. This is simply because what we are is there revealed so continuously; because the relationships are so constant, so intimate; because we are in such an interdependent state that our independent selfish ways prove entirely inadequate to the task. This is exactly why marriage is such a divinely sanctifying, growth-producing institution as a supreme crucible in life. Selfish living simply has no place in it.

But selfishness or sin may, if we so choose, shock us into an awakening and a development of these higher faculties, which have previously been asleep. The opportunity to partake of the sacrament on the Sabbath day out of the broken heart and contrite spirit gives us a renewal in divine scripts. It charges our batteries again with a sense of who we really are, and what life is about, and how sacred marriage and family life is, and who Christ is, and how important it is to get the Spirit so that we can follow him and become capable of living as a family with him and our

Father in Heaven throughout eternity. In the very moment when we are handed our cross, if we could briefly view the death of Christ, as Jacob put it (Jacob 1:8), or watch with him and pray that we enter not into this temptation, as Jesus counseled his three disciples (Matthew 26:41), and then follow the Spirit's directive, we could rise above old inadequate scripts and slowly, perhaps imperceptibly, but literally create a heaven on earth.

There is wisdom in the saying from the Eastern tradition, "By what they fall, by that they rise."

The cross we are handed daily, perhaps even hourly, is the test of our highest human/divine faculty, our agency, our power to choose. If we do follow him we will rise, if we don't we will fall. If we fall we can learn and rise up again. Our weakness can become our strength. "And if men come unto me I will show unto them their weakness that they may be humble; and my grace is sufficient for all men that humble themselves before me; for if they humble themselves before me, and have faith in me, then will I make weak things become strong unto them. . . . And because thou hast seen thy weakness thou shalt be made strong, even unto the sitting down in the place which I have prepared in the mansions of my Father." (Ether 12:27, 37.)

Couples need not be discouraged by bad feeling or a bad situation but can turn it to the Lord's advantage and let him use it to their good.

When One Loses the Spirit

Perhaps the most difficult testing moment comes when one spouse loses the Spirit through personal transgression and apostasy. The other spouse—say, the wife—is disillusioned and heartbroken. She can't understand it. She tries to stay faithful but her faith is tested and shaken, even her faith in herself. Her emotions circle from anger to bitterness to guilt to hopelessness to fear and back to anger, and so forth. Her life ebbs away. Many roads could be taken—self-justification, social validation, counseling with uninspired sources, punishing her husband in various ways, turning the children against him, moving closer to the Church but further from the gospel, and so on. Or she may turn on herself, taking all the blame for the alienation of affection. Or she may join her husband in transgression in order to keep him or to punish him.

Alternatively she may take another road—rocky, difficult, less traveled, hard to see: the divine one. In following Christ she would carry a cross daily. But she would realize what she was doing and he would comfort, strengthen, and inspire her through the Holy Ghost. The Lord, in his matchless ways—including assigning guardian angels—would watch after her and compensate for many deficiencies in her marriage and family life.

She would stay close to the Church and her priesthood leaders and very close to the Lord and his holy gospel. She would counsel with inspired sources. She would ask her husband to give her a blessing or for him to arrange for priesthood teachers and leaders to do it. Instead of turning on her husband or herself with condemnation she would turn to the Lord and then to her husband. Without either damning him or condoning his behavior she would affirm her belief in his basic potential and goodness and patiently show him unconditional love. She would look on him with compassion rather than accusation—seeing and treating him as an investigator—knowing that punishing him for his transgression will only make him feel justified in his own darkened mind. And in that darkened reasoning he'll actually want to be punished, and even speak and behave to get more of it—for if he feels he has atoned for his own sins through her punishment, he will justify himself in not feeling the need for the Savior's atonement.

Obviously, to take such an approach would require her turning fully to the Lord. This is the essence of true repentance and her highest growth. As she completes such repentance she will not suffer, in the spiritual sense, from his sins against her. (D&C 19:16.) Such Christlike love may eventually bring him to his senses, because with the Lord as her advocate, all that is good within him will be appealed to by the Spirit of Christ within. Her modeling will shepherd him to the True Shepherd. Her faithful love—the fruit of the Spirit—will midwife his second birth process.

And if he doesn't turn about—for he has his agency—she will have peace in her sadness. Perhaps stewardships may need to be reassigned, but she will not be bitter. She will continue to seek his growth and happiness and acknowledge with gratitude the Lord's hand in all things. And in the long run nothing important will be denied her. She will have the fullness of eternity.

"By what they fall, by that they rise."

29

Seven Sources of Internal Security

Most people derive their security from external sources—that is, from the environment, possessions, or the opinions of others, including one's spouse. The fundamental problem with any external source is dependency on those sources, which means that our lives become buffeted and made uncertain and insecure by whatever happens to those sources.

We need to cultivate dependency, or better still interdependency, upon a source that is constant and faithful regardless of circumstances. The ability to rescript our lives and to stay with these new divine scripts will require a great deal of courage. Courage arises out of deep internal sense of personal worth, personal value, and personal security. President Harold B. Lee defined courage as "the quality of every quality at its highest testing point." Such testing points are the times when the crosses are handed to us, and it does indeed take courage to carry them and follow Christ.

Consider seven sources which are independent of circumstance or opinion. I sincerely believe that if people will cultivate these seven sources regularly, almost imperceptibly within them will grow a sense of personal worth and security, independent of upbringing, circumstance, and opinion. With such independent strength, they are capable of choosing to be interdependent, particularly in their highest stewardship in life—that of marriage and family life.

The Divine Source

The most fundamental source and the root of all the rest, one which can absolutely be relied on in any given set of circumstances, is our relationship with each member of the Godhead. "We believe in God, the Eternal Father, and in His Son Jesus Christ, and in the Holy Ghost" (third article of faith). When our lives are founded or centered on God and Christ through the Holy Ghost, everything else works together for our good.

> And now, my sons, remember, remember that it is upon the rock of our Redeemer, who is Christ, the Son of God, that ye must build your foundation; that when the devil shall send forth his mighty winds, yea, his shafts in the whirlwind, yea, when all his hail and his mighty storm shall beat upon you, it shall have no power over you to drag you down to the gulf of misery and endless wo, because of the rock upon which ye are built, which is a sure foundation, a foundation whereon if men build they cannot fall. (Helaman 5:12.)

To build our lives on this divine source means cultivating the mind of God within us so that we are embodying divine scripts; emulating the model of Jesus Christ, using his church as the proper pattern for organizing and directing our family life; seeing the temple as the perfect pattern for our own homes. This means constantly educating and obeying our conscience until it becomes so sensitive that we can and will live under the influence of the Holy Spirit. The more we do these things, the greater will be our happiness and growth in marriage, and the more we will be given wisdom and guidance and power in solving or transcending the various problems and challenges we encounter.

What about secular marriage counseling? Does that play a role? If two people are struggling at a telestial level in their marriage, counseling might significantly help them reach the point at which they can communicate and from which they can thus move toward what we might call a terrestial level. I know there is a growing body of extremely competent, gospel-oriented professional counselors who continually strive to integrate revealed and discovered knowledge in their thinking and practice. They eventually point to gospel solutions, knowing that the movement from the terrestial to the celestial is fundamentally a process of building our lives upon our Father in Heaven and his Son, Jesus Christ. As we yoke up to their work, every other yoke can be broken, including the yoke of ignorance and fear and contention.

The rest of the six sources of internal security flow directly or indirectly out of this divine one.

Rich Private Life

Cultivate the habit of private meditation and contemplation. This could be joined with prayer and with studying and searching the scriptures. Many people are bored when they are by themselves, because their lives have been a merry-go-round of activity, almost always with other people. Cultivate the ability to be alone and to think deeply, to "do nothing," to enjoy silence and solitude. Reflect, write, listen, plan, visualize, ponder, relax.

You can ask anyone who has a rich private life how important and precious it is to his sense of personal worth and security. And you will sense there is absolutely no reservation in his mind about it. The Savior, again, is a perfect model, for he continually went apart for prayer, meditation, preparation, and planning.

Appreciate Nature

Again, check with anyone who becomes deeply immersed in the beauties of nature, especially in the mountains or at the seashore—particularly early in the morning or in the evening or very late at night. In nature, God can be seen moving in all his majesty, and his magnificent creation will filter its quiet beauty and strength into your soul. It is almost like being given a fresh tank of oxygen. Nature is one of the divine scripting sources and teaches many beautiful things. Nature teaches us God's processes.

Test it for yourself by simply using your memory. Think of a vacation or outing you have had, one into nature, where you were close to the earth and experienced quiet times in beautiful settings such as canyons, lakes, rivers, streams, seashores, or high mountains. What did you feel when you returned back to normal life? What were you like? Were you not more contemplative, more inwardly peaceful and tranquil and quiet, and less in need of returning to the frantic "rat-race"? Were you not more able to sidestep negative energy?

Now think of another vacation, one filled with a lot of fun but also with schedules and rush and travel and socials, times spent at carnivals, circuses, amusement parks, or whatever. What were you like when you returned from that vacation or outing? Were you not exhausted and spent and frazzled? perhaps eager to tell everyone about the fun-filled times you had and things you did and places you went to, but still feeling in need of a real vacation when you returned?

Sharpen Your Saw

Cultivate the habit of sharpening your saw physically, mentally, and spiritually every day. We talked about the spiritual side in the first two sources, so let's focus on the physical and the mental. Cultivate the habit of regular exercise at least every other day in stretching, aerobic, and toning exercises. Weekend exercise isn't enough; in fact, some studies show it hurts us more than helps us, because of overdoing it. And our bodies, particularly as we grow older, haven't the flexibility and resiliency to deal with those weekend stresses.

Studies are showing that one of the finest exercises is walking. This can be part of a rich private life as well—while walking we can think and plan and reflect and enjoy nature. It doesn't put the wrong kind of stress on the body, but if we do it vigorously and long enough we will stress the body in appropriate ways so as to strengthen the cardiovascular system and enlarge our capacity to process oxygen.

Regular, vigorous exercise is vital to radiant health and unquestionably influences not just the quantity of our years but the quality of the life in those years.

For mental exercise, I suggest cultivating the habit of reading. Read widely and broadly and deeply. If you live near colleges, universities, or technical schools, take a course now and then. If you are not near one, sign up for a correspondence course so that there is some external discipline and accountability procedure. Cut way back on television. Read history, biography, autobiography, good fiction—all the great literature. I suggest you spend at least seven hours a week on this kind of reading.

When we continue our education, our abilities to think, communicate, and learn are being continually developed. Then our economic security is not as dependent upon our jobs, our boss's opinion, or human institutions, but rather upon our ability to produce. The great unseen job market is called "unsolved problems," and there are always many vacancies for those who exercise initiative and learn how to create value for themselves by showing how they essentially represent solutions to these problems. The typical unemployed person merely is another problem to a prospective employer. I am convinced that a person can get just about any job he wants, where he wants to get it, if he will be proactive and take the initiative and responsibility to research the particular problems the prospective employing institutions are facing, and then learn how to present his experience, interests, and skills as meeting those problems.

There are two excellent books on this very subject: *What Color Is Your Parachute?* by Richard Bolles, and *Executive Jobs Unlimited* by Carl Boll. Employed people who take the course of least resistance and refuse to sharpen the saw will not only find that their saw speed slows down; eventually they will become obsolete and increasingly dependent upon playing it safe in the employing institution. They will become protective, political minded, and security minded—wearing the golden handcuffs.

By continuing to sharpen the saw mentally and upgrading our skills, our knowledge, and our problem-solving capacities—and above all, our ability to continue to learn—we will become economically independent. Economic independence does not mean being independently wealthy; it merely means that we know we have the power to produce wealth if we need to and we're not dependent upon our present job or our boss's opinion of us.

We must simply commit ourselves that we will never get too busy sawing that we don't take time to sharpen the saw. Then we'll *"make* it a good day."

Give Service

Anonymous service is particularly important. The Savior's incomparable philosophy that we will find our life when we lose it in his service is a totally true paradox. If our intent is to serve, to bless others, without self-concern, a byproduct of our service comes within—a kind of psychological, emotional, spiritual reward in the form of internal security and peace. Such a reward comes in the second mile of our callings, whether the callings come direct from the Spirit or through the priesthood. To paraphrase Matthew 6:1-4, "He that does his alms before men has already received his reward. He that does it in secret shall receive his reward in the open."

Show Integrity

When we are true to the light we have been given, when we keep our word on a consistent basis, when we are continually striving to harmonize our habit system with our value system, then our life is integrated together. Our honor becomes greater than our moods, and we can have confidence in ourselves because we know ourselves and know that we will be true and faithful under temptation. The Lord indicated that his honor is his power (Moses 4:1,3). This will also be true with us. Integrity is the foundation of all true goodness and greatness. The internal security which emerges from it eliminates the need to live for impression, to exaggerate for effect, to drop names or places, to borrow strength from credentials or possessions or fashions or affiliations or associations or status symbols. When we wear God's divine armor we have no need for cynicism or sarcasm or cutting humor. Our sense of humor becomes spontaneous, healthy, and proportionate to the situation.

> Therefore whosoever heareth these sayings of mine, and doeth them, I will liken him unto a wise man, which built his house upon a rock:
> And the rain descended, and the floods came, and the winds blew, and beat upon that house; and it fell not: for it was founded upon a rock.
> And every one that heareth these sayings of mine, and doeth them not, shall be likened unto a foolish man, which built his house upon the sand:
> And the rain descended, and the floods came, and the winds blew, and beat upon that house; and it fell: and great was the fall of it. (Matthew 7:24-27.)

That Other Person

The final source of security I feel particularly strong about (and I am sure there are many others) is *another person* who loves us and believes in us even when we don't believe in ourselves. In a sense this source is external to oneself and imperfect. Perhaps it shouldn't rate an equal place with the other six sources, all of which are relatively independent of the fickle forces of life. So why should I mention it here? Because *there are* those people who are true and faithful and are so inwardly anchored and secured and rooted that we can depend upon them. Not in the ultimate sense, as we need to depend upon the Lord, but perhaps in the more proximate sense. They know us, they care about us, their love is unconditional, and they will stay with us when everyone else deserts us, particularly when we desert ourselves.

I believe that a good percentage of mothers have unconditional love toward their children; perhaps a lower percentage of the fathers. Maybe it's what the mother went through to bring the child into the world that gives her such an unconditional love and a continuing belief in the basic goodness and potential of her son or daughter. Those who are divinely centered also possess the same capacity. Such individuals can make all the difference in our lives.

Think of your own life. Did you ever run into a teacher, a leader, a neighbor, a friend, a coach, an advisor who believed in you when you didn't believe in yourself? One who stayed with you regardless? Not someone who was soft and permissive with you, someone who gave in to you, but someone who would not give *in* to you but neither would give *up* on you. I have asked this question to audiences all over the country and find that about one-third to one-half of the people respond positively—that they know what I mean.

The Shakespearean sonnet reproduced below may represent our common experience with such people. Use your imagination and study each line. Think about each line, and the meaning in the sonnet will grow within you. You will also come to sense just how important that one person—that "sweet love remembered" —is to you. It's one of the most basic themes in great literature and great theatre and good movies.

> When in disgrace with fortune and men's eyes,
> I all alone beweep my outcast state,
> And trouble deaf heaven with my bootless cries,
> And look upon myself and curse my fate,
> Wishing me like to one more rich in hope,
> Featur'd like him, like him with friends possess'd,
> Desiring this man's art, and that man's scope,
> With what I most enjoy contented least;
> Yet in these thoughts myself almost despising,
> Haply I think on thee, and then my state,
> Like to the lark at break of day arising
> From sullen earth, sings hymns at heaven's gate;
> > For thy sweet love remember'd such wealth brings
> > That then I scorn to change my state with kings.

To me, the thrilling challenge is the awareness of how we can be such a person to other people. Whenever we sense someone is at the crossroads in life, let's resolve and do whatever is necessary in going the second mile and in communicating to him that we believe in him, that we will not give up on him, that we love him regardless of his past failures or his present behavior or his reputation with others. When he knows this love is trustworthy, we can also be very bold with him in letting him know how unacceptable certain behaviors are. We can be so bold as to say that we won't tolerate it anymore, that we think more of him, that he is capable of much more. Since the person's emotional bank account with us is high, we can be far more bold than we would ever dare be with others in whose bank we have deposited little.

Six Ways of Showing Love

I believe that if we would love people in six ways, almost simultaneously, such love would greatly increase their capacity to receive the light and knowledge they have been given. The six ways are: (1) be a genuine friend, constantly extend the hand of fellowship; (2) pray with them and for them; (3) listen to them with true empathy—in other words, receive them to yourself; (4) share with them what you have to give, to teach and to testify; (5) affirm them, believe in them, encourage them; (6) walk with them, sacrifice for them, go the second mile for them, do things they would never expect you to do.

This kind of love must be received in order to be given. It is a "fruit of the Spirit." Perhaps we receive it in the same six or more ways we give it, through deep spiritual/emotional identification with how the Lord truly loved and loves us in these ways. ("I am the Way.")

Full Circle

In discussing love we find ourselves coming full circle. Love is the beginning and the end of our exploration of marriage and family life. T. S. Eliot sums it up: "We shall not cease from exploration, and the end of all our exploring will be to arrive where we started and to know the place for the first time."

True love is a "fruit of the Spirit" and comes from surrendering first our selfishness and then our hearts to God. Such divine leverage magnifies all of life. In the words of President Ezra Taft Benson:

> Men and women who turn their lives over to God will find out that he can make a lot more out of their lives than they can. He will deepen their joys, expand their vision, quicken their minds, strengthen their muscles, lift their spirits, multiply their blessings, increase their opportunities, comfort their souls, raise up friends, and pour out peace. Whoever will lose his life to God will find he has eternal life.

Index

A—

Abba (title), 16
Abortion, Judaic view, 11
Abundance mentality, 178-79
Accommodation, marital, 144
Accountability, 174, 180
Actions, causes, 60
Activity trap, 194
Adam and Eve, 72
Adoption, law of, 8-9
Adultery, 221-23
Adversary, 202
Affection, 58
Affliction, meaning in, 38
Agreement, 178
Attitudes, predetermined, 159
Authoritarianism, 149-50, 152, 188
Autobiographical listening, 199

B—

Balance, 118
Barrenness, Judaic view, 14
Behavior, causes, 60
  change, 75
Bitterness, 61
Blaming mode, 141
Blunderers, 101-2
Body, 110-11, 113
Body language, 204
Boldness, 232
Brain dominance theory, 130-33, 203-4
Brown, Hugh B., 74

C—

Callings, Church, 52, 56, 151
Cannon, George Q., on family
  kinships, 7
Capitulation, 174-75
Celestial kingdom, glory, 8
Celibacy, Judaic view, 11-12
Change, 125, 143
Cheerleaders, 163-65
Child rearing, 150-51
Childhood, life-shaping experiences, 99

Children, divine conception, 159-60
  problems, 153-58
  rebelliousness, 143
  teaching, to pray, 158-66
Children of Judah, 10
Choices, 60
Chores, assignment, 182
Christlike love, 30-32
Church, divine model, 109
  instrument to glorify family, 52
  mission, 148
Circumstances, tests of, 33-40
Comfort zone, 135-36, 147
Commitment, in marriage, 27-28
Communication, channels, 204
  nonverbal, 203
  one-on-one, 167-69
Communication skill, 198-208
Compassion, 71
Competence, conscious and
  unconscious, 101-2
Competence problems, 154-57
Complementariness, 210-11
Compromise, 217
Conditional love, 114-16
Conflict, marital, 76-78
Conjugal love, 25
Conscience, 165-66
Consequences, 180
  management, 157-58
Content, communication, 204
Convergent problems, 213
Convergent thinkers, 217
Conversion, 150, 175
Core values, 200
Corrections, with love, 70
Counterdependence, 142
Courage, 224
Courtesy, 71
Creation, ultimate meaning, 5
Creative problem solving, 217, 219
Cross, daily, 219-21

D—

Damnation, 61
Darkness, opposite of love, 21

Dating, married couples, 72
Death, fear of, 8
Dedication of homes, 47-48
Defensive minds, 212
Delegation, 122-23, 182-88
Dependence, emotional, 142
Determinism, 100
Diagnosis, 133
Diets, 116
Difference resolution, 211-14
Differences, personal, 105-7, 176-78
  valuing, 210-11
Disagreement, 178
Discipline, 150, 173
Divergent problems, 213-16, 218
Divine knowledge, 159-60
Divine scripts, 225
"Divine sparks," 10
Divorce, 83

E—

Earth, creation of, 5
Economic independence, 229
Education, continuance, 228
Effectiveness, 124
Efficiency, 124
Elijah, spirit of, 63-65
Elopement, 46-47
Emotional bank account, 113-17, 175-76,
  204-5
Empathic listening, 205-7
Employment, 228
Enemies, love of, 82-83
Environment, and heredity, 60
Eternal family, 5
Eternal life, aspirational strivings, 4, 7-8
Eternal marriage, 46-47
Eternal perspective, importance, 95-96
  mortal aspect, 97
Ethos, 133
Eve, Judaic view, 12-13
Evil, 59
Exaltation, 52
Example. See Modeling
Executive Jobs Unlimited, 228
Exercise, 227
Expectations, commitment regarding,
  180
Experience, firsthand, 45

F—

Faculties, higher, 219-20
Family, divine principles, 145-47
  eternal, 5
  goals, 149
  intergenerational relationships, 144
  Judaic teachings, 10-14
  lack of warmth, 144
  low priority, 196
Family council, 171-72
Family counseling, 96
Family exaltation, 52-53
Family governance, 54, 152, 170
Family home evening, 171-72
Family organization, Church model, 145
Family prayer, 158-59, 161-62
Father-son relationship, 113-14
Fathers, hearts turned to, 65
Feeling, union of, 43
Feelings, control, 59-60
  ranking, 170
  surveying, 54
Fire, love is, 22-23
Fitness, personal, 113
Forgiveness, 78-83
Freedom, 38, 59-60
Friday date night, 72
Fulness of the priesthood, 86

G—

Getting to Yes, 212
Goal setting, 147-49
Goal/value conflicts. See Value/goal
  conflicts
Goals, Church, 148
  correct principles, 149
  production, 112
God, image, 10
  needs love, 25-26
Godhead, different roles, 126
Gospel principles, marital foundation,
  75-76
Gratitude, 39-40
Grievances, 79
Group settings, 168
Guide for the Perplexed, A, 212-13
Guidelines, 180

H—

Habits, 193
Handedness, 131
Happiness, sources, 59
Heart, 136, 165
Hebrew language, no neuter case, 10
Hereafter, 84
Heredity, and environment, 60
Hitler, Adolph, 82-83
Holy Ghost, enlivens senses, 83
Holy Spirit of Promise, 64-65
Home, Judaic view, 13-14
Homes, dedicated, 47-48
Honor, 229
Housecleaning, 128
Hugs, 70
Humility, 102
  of speech, 202
Humor, 73
Hypothesis formation, 135

I—

Ideal vs. real, 98
Imagination, 136
Immaturity, 142
Importance, 192
Impulses, control, 59-60
Incompetence, conscious and
  unconscious, 101-2
Increase, cause, 53
Independence, 141, 143
Influence, 119
Ingratitude, 40
Integrity, 229
Intent, communication, 203-4
Interdependence, 141, 143
Invulnerability, 171

J—

Jacob's well, 15-16
Jesus Christ, miracles, 17-19
  parables, 19
  role model, 104-5, 108, 225
  teachings on family, 15-17
Judaism, teachings on family, 10-14
Justice, 80-81
Justice/mercy struggle, 214

K—

Kimball, Heber C., correspondence with
  wife, 88-89
Kindness, 71

L—

Labels, 202
Laziness, 102
Leader role, 125
Leaders, brain dominance, 131-32
  change, 143
  interdependent, 143
  producer activity, 127
Leadership, 150
Left brain dominance, 131, 135-36
Life scripts. *See* Scripting
Light, 23
  God-centeredness, 21
Lightheartedness, 73
Listening, autobiographical, 199
  empathic, 205-7
  key, 171
  reflective, 207
  risks, 200
  "Little things," 70-74
Logic, language, 203
Logos, 133
Loneliness, 66
Lose/win situations, 175
Love, fallen out of, 23-24
  from God, 20-21
  is fire, 22-23
  knowledge perfects, 3-5
  lawful, 23
  reciprocation, 31
  "ripple effect," 31
  self-generating, 23
  shining thing, 21
  showing, 232-33
  unconditional, 30-32, 114-16, 142
  unfeigned, 55
Lust, 59

M—

McKay, David O., 72, 117
Male stereotypes, 131
Man, Deity within, 53

Management, involvement principle, 152
Manager role, 121-24
Managers, absence, 140
  brain dominance, 131-32
  interdependent, 143
Manipulative techniques, 117, 179
Maps, personal, 199
Marriage, balance, 56
  challenges, 85
  commitment, 27-28
  continual courtship, 117
  divine goals, 148-49
  foundation, 75-76
  God-ordained, 5
  ideal possibilities, 4
  Jesus' teachings, 15-17
  Judaic teachings, 11, 13
  little things, 70-74
  manipulative behavior, 117
  one-on-one communication, 169
  physical union, 24-25
  problem solving, 59-60
  selfishness, 61
  tests of circumstances, 33
  vulnerability, 200
Marriage counseling, 76, 96, 225-26
Marriage encounter movement, 202-3
Marriage problems, brain dominance
    example, 133-35
  resolution, 75-78
Married couples, conflict, 76-78
  counselor relationship, 54
  date night, 72
  depth of love, 28-29
  redeemers, 48-49
  togetherness/apartness, 56
  transgression, 221-23
Martyr role, 175
Mate selection, 8
Mechanical prayer, 160-61
Meetings, family, 171-72
Mental exercise, 228
Mental imagery, 136
Mentors, 108-9
Methods orientation, 124
Mimicry, 207
Miracles, of Christ, 17-19
Mission, decision to serve, 114-16
Modeling, 100, 103, 166
  See also Role models
Mortal perspective, 96-97
Mothers, 55

Motivation, 132
Motivational problems, 154, 157
Mountain men, 141
Murder, Judaic view, 11
Mutuality, marital, 77

N—

Nagging, 119, 188
Natural affections, 58
Nature, appreciation, 226-27
  divine model, 110-11
Needs, and wants, 163
Non-productive nature, 140
Nuclear family, 63

O—

Obesity, 116
Offices, Church, 52
"One-on-one" communication, 167-69
Open-heartedness, 178
Opinions, of others, 200
Opportunity mindedness, 192
Others, significant, 230-31

P—

Pain, 37
Parables, of Christ, 19
Parents, job delegation, 182-88
  producer behavior, 123
  role models, 99-100, 128-29
  steadfastness, 142
  teaching/training, 153-66
Pathos, 133
Peace, 31, 90-91
Perception, 201-3
Permissiveness, 174-75
Personal differences, 105-7, 176-78
Personality building, 32
Personnel management, 152
Perversions, 58
Phone calls, 193
Physical creation, divine model, 110-11
Physical differences, 210
Physical fitness, 227
Planning, 147-49
Positions, Church, 52
Positive Mental Attitude (PMA), 137
Posterity, 11
Power, corruptions, 55

Pratt, Orson, on love and knowledge, 3-4
Pratt, Parley P., eternal family vision, 3-4
  on natural affections, 58
  on spirit communication, 67
Prayer, answers, 163-65
  commitment, 162
  conflict resolution, 78
  heartfelt, 161
  levels, 160
  morning, 159
  personal, 162, 169
  teaching children, 158-66
  teaching moment, 162-63
  two-way, 164-66
  See also Family prayer
Precepts, 100
Prejudgment, 171
Premortal life, 5-6
Priesthood, fulness, 86
  instrument to glorify family, 52
Principles, abstractions, 100
  correct, 181
  ease of teachings, 105
Priorities, 169-70
  establishment, 192, 194, 197
  resetting, 195-96
Private life, 226
Proactive manner, 194, 228
Problem definition, 106
Problem-mindedness, 192
Problem solving, interactive, 209-10
  self-directed, 59-60
  synergistic, 216-19
Problems, diagnosis, 154
  self-help, 76
Producer role, 121-24
Producers, independent nature, 141, 143
Production capability, 112-13, 126
Production lack, 141
Provocations, 219
Psychic space, 202
Psychological contract, 182-88
"Put-downs," 70

Q—

Queen of the Sabbath, 12

R—

Reading, 228
Realization, 165

Rebellion, parental effect, 143
Redeemers, married couples, 48-49
Reflective listening, 207
Reflective thinking, 213
Repentance, modeling, 103
Reproof, 151
Rescripting, 136-39
Resentments, 79, 175
Resources, to aid stewardship, 180
Responses, 59-60
  pre-determined, 159
Results, desired, 180
Resurrected bodies, 84
Revenge, 176
Right brain dominance, 131, 135-36
"Ripple effect," love, 31
Role expectations, 105
Role models, 99-100
Role play, 169
Roles. *See* Leader role; Manager role;
  Producer role
Ruach (Hebrew word), 12
Rule (term), 54

S—

Sabbath, Judaic view, 12
Sacrament, 220
Sacrifice, 85-86
Sadat, Anwar, on inner change, 138-39
Satisfaction, 165
Scarcity mentality, 178-79
Schechinah, 10
Script conflicts, 105-7
Scripting, 220
  component percentages, 104
  people-induced, 99-100, 104
  See also Rescripting
Scripting models, divine, 108
Scripture (term), 100
Scriptures, identification with, 104
Sealing, 64-65, 88-89
Security, inner, 171, 200
  sources, 224
Security base, 201
Self, giving of, 55
Self-awareness, 213, 219
Self-determination, 100
Self-esteem, 113
Self-improvement literature, 137
Self-knowledge, 58
Self-management, 191

Selfish living, 220
Selfishness, divine, 61-62
  marital, 60-61
Senses, 83
Sentiment, language, 203
Service, anonymous, 229
Sex characteristics, eternal, 5
Shabbat eve, 13
Sharing, authentic, 208
Sinful affections, 58
Single people, Judaic view, 14
  never-married, 49-50
Slavery, 61
Smith, Joseph, leadership, 189
Snow, Eliza R., 69
Snow, Lorenzo, on ambition, 52
  on mothers, 55
  on potential for godhood, 51
Solitude, 226
"Soul-mate," 8
Sounds, 204
Speech, manner of, 201
Spirit, loss of, 221-23
Spirit of Elijah, 63-65
Spirit of the Lord, 7, 23, 85
Spirit world, 66-68, 85
Stakes, reorganization, 151
Stewardship, 173, 183-84, 187-88
Stewardship/discipline system, 180-81
Still small voice, 165
Subordination, 170
Success literature, 137-38
Suffering, meaning in, 37-39
Suicide, folklore belief, 8
Supervision in Teaching (manual), 189
Surrogate parenting, 68
Sympathy, 205
Synergistic problem solving, 216-19
Systems orientation, 124

T—

Talmage, James E., on eternity of sex, 5
  on priesthood and women, 53
Teaching, 153-66, 181
  by example, 160
  divine, 41
Teenagers, counterdependent role, 142
Telephone calls, 193
Temple, model home, 109-10
  purposes, 41-47
Temple marriage, 46-47

Temple work, visualization, 136-37
Testimony, 175
Testing points, 224
Thought process, 96
Time management, 191-93
Time use, 119-20
Trade-offs, 193-94
Training solutions, 153-66
Training systems, 128
Translation problem, 198-99
Trust, 71
Trust levels, 132, 204-5
Truth, 5

U—

Unconditional love, 30-32, 114-16, 160
Understanding, empathic, 206
  giving, 178
  mutual, 170, 180
Unemployed persons, 228
Unforgiveness, 78-83
Unmarried people, 49-50
Unrighteous dominion, 54
Urgency, 192-94

V—

Value/goal conflicts, 106
Value problems, 154, 157
Valuing differences, 210-11
Vengeance, 176
Vindictiveness, 176
Vision, the, 4
Visualization, 136, 220
Vulnerability, 171, 200

W—

Walking, 227
Wants, and needs, 163
What Color Is Your Parachute? 228
Whitney, Orson F., on premortal
  acquaintances, 8
Win/win principle, 174-79, 210
Woman, Judaic view, 12-13
Women, eventually to reign, 53
  power struggles, 55
Woodruff, Wilford, on laws of
  adoption, 9
Words, 204

Y—

Yard maintenance, 128, 182-87
Yelling, 159
Yin-Yang elements, 133
Young, Brigham, on ability for
    increase, 53
  visionary man, 84

Z—

Zion, definition, 141